WITCHES
& HISTORIANS
"INTERPRETATIONS OF SALEM"

WITCHES & HISTORIANS
INTERPRETATIONS OF SALEM

Edited by **Marc Mappen**
Rutgers University

ROBERT E. KRIEGER PUBLISHING COMPANY
HUNTINGTON, NEW YORK
1980

Original edition 1980

Printed and Published by
ROBERT E. KRIEGER PUBLISHING COMPANY, INC.
645 NEW YORK AVENUE
HUNTINGTON, NEW YORK 11743

Printed in the United States of America

Library of Congress Cataloging in Publication Data

Mappen, Marc.
    Witches and historians: Interpretations of Salem
    1. Witchcraft—Massachusetts—Salem—Addresses, es-
says, lectures.   2. Salem, Mass.—History—Addresses, essays, lectures. I. Title.
BF1576.M34   974.4'5   78-2579
ISBN 0-88275-653-2

Contents

Introduction

The trial and execution of a handful of alleged witches in Salem, Massachusetts in 1692 has been one of the most exhaustively studied episodes in American history. Certainly, as much has been written about Salem as about the landing of the Mayflower or the signing of the Declaration of Independence. And yet the events of 1692 did not lead to the establishment of a new colony or to the destruction of an empire. By any measure it was a relatively minor episode of the American colonial era.

Why then has Salem received so much attention? One reason is its stark drama: the shrieks of the afflicted girls, the testimonies to the existence of demons and witches by sober farmers, and the jolting of the cart on gallows hill—these images have a fascination that transcends the dry, seventeenth century prose that documents this period. And then there is the utter mystery of the affair: why did this tragedy so suddenly engulf an outwardly peaceful New England village? In America, a nation founded on the enlightened ideals of reason and progress, this question has been particularly disturbing. This book is a survey of the ways in which Americans have attempted to explain the problem of Salem over a span of three centuries.

Even before the last witch had been hanged, New Englanders were debating the nature of the evidence against the accused. In the face of mounting criticism of the trials, Cotton Mather attempted to prove that the witches were genuinely in league with Satan (see section 3). But Mather's was a losing position. Within short period of time observers, such as the Rev. John Hale, came to the belief that they had made a tragic mistake (see selection 5); and Mather himself became the object of harsh criticism from the Boston merchant Robert Calef (see selection 4).

But if Satan had not walked in Salem, how could the tragedy be explained? In 1867, Charles W. Upham offered an explanation that seemed logical and convincing. According to Upham, the so-called "afflicted girls" who were the principal witnesses against the witches, had deliberately lied. This conspiracy thesis became the standard interpretation, and was echoed in the history text books of the nineteenth century (see selection 6).

The problem of Salem had not been settled, however, and succeeding generations of historians tinkered with aspects of this interpretation. One such aspect pertained to the mental state of the principal actors. Had the afflicted girls been lying, or were they actually the victims of some sort of hysteria? Among the many writers who tried to answer this question was Ernest Caulfield, who argued that the rigors of Puritan childrearing contributed to the unstable personalities of the Salem girls (see selection 8). More recently the biologist Linnda Caporael has argued that the irrational behavior of the girls was caused by the spread of a disease (see selection 9). Caporael's diagnosis, in turn, has been disputed by two psychologists, Nicholas P. Spanos and Jack Gottlieb (see selection 10).

Another contention arose that held Puritan leaders and Puritan beliefs responsible for the tragedy. Charles Lyman Kittredge felt that the men and women of Massachusetts should not be singled out for blame, since the belief in witchcraft was common throughout the seventeenth century world (see selection 11).

What of the witches themselves? It has been suggested that the Salem jury was not entirely wrong; that some of the accused had actually tried to harm their neighbors by using black magic. This is the conclusion of one modern historian, Chadwick Hansen (see selection 7).

But if writers over the past three hundred years have differed over matters of interpretation, most of them have shared a common preoccupation with the question of guilt. In a sense, they have taken over the role of the Salem judges and have extended the search for the guilty party away from Satan and toward other culprits—the girls, the Puritans, hysteria, or disease.

One exception was the historian Perry Miller. In writing *The New England Mind,* Miller was concerned with reconstructing the framework of Puritan beliefs, and he attempted to show how the events of Salem fit into that framework (see selection 12). In recent years, other historians have followed Miller's lead. They have studied witchcraft not as an aberration, but as a reflection of larger themes in the mind and the social order of colonial America. John Demos, for example, has used the subject of witchcraft to make bold assumptions about the subconscious motivation of New Englanders (see selection 13). Kai T. Erikson has used the Puritans' persecution of the witches as an example of how societies react to internal disorder (see selection 14). Paul Boyer and Stephen Nissenbaum have suggested that the Salem tragedy was one episode in the decay of a traditional way of life (see selection 15).

The same shift in perspective can be seen in the writings of historians of European witchcraft. One need only contrast an essay on witchcraft written by John Fiske in the early twentieth century (see selection 1) with a 1971 essay by Lawrence Stone (see selection 2) to see how our understanding of witchcraft has broadened.

Why has the interpretation of witchcraft changed so dramatically? There are a number of interrelated reasons. First, historians have begun to broaden their scope beyond the traditional concern with great men and great events. There is an increased desire to understand the everyday lives of ordinary men and women within their families and communities. Because witchcraft was a phenomenon acted out on the village level, involving people on the lowest rung of the social ladder, it provides insights into everyday life. Second, historians are increasingly receptive to the findings of other disciplines, such as sociology and anthropology. The latter subject, in particular, has developed a vast amount of literature on witchcraft that is rich in suggestions for historical study. Third, historians seem to be more receptive, or perhaps more inured to the persistence of irrationality in human affairs. In view of the present century, marked by violence and persecution on a scale far greater than that which was visited on the witches, it is no longer so easy to believe in the inevitable march of progress, reason, and justice. As one historian, Marion L. Starkey, put it, "who in my day has a right to be indignant with people in Salem of 1692?"

It is evident that recent research has revolutionized our understanding of this seventeenth century tragedy. Perhaps this is testimony to a new vigor in historical inquiry. Whatever the reason for this change in the historian's approach, it is clear that the chronicle of events in this little New England village continue to fascinate and challenge the imagination and intellect.

* * *

Before we turn to the historical writings on witchcraft in Salem, let us briefly examine the events themselves.

The period of the witchcraft episode was a difficult one for Massachusetts. In a series of convulsions, the old charter, which had provided a measure of independence for the colony, was revoked by England and a new and more restrictive form of government was imposed. It was at about this time that convulsions of a different sort occurred in the household of Samuel Parris, the minister of Salem Village.* Parris' daughter and his niece were afflicted by severe fits and other strange symptoms. A doctor who had been summoned to treat the two girls concluded that they were bewitched.

---

*Salem Village, where the outbreak occurred, is now Danvers, Massachusetts. The trials and executions took place in neighboring Salem Town, now called Salem.

Earlier incidents of witchcraft had occurred in New England. Only four years before a witch had been hanged for casting an evil spell on the children of a family in Boston. Thus it was quite possible for Salem residents to accept the idea that witchcraft lay behind this latest trouble. Three women from the lowest rank of Salem society were accused: Sarah Good, Sarah Osborn, and the slave of the Rev. Parris, Tituba. In the course of her interrogation by the magistrates, Tituba confessed that she was truly a witch: she had harmed the children, she had flown through the air, and she had added her name to Satan's book.

From this point, as the authorities attempted to discover Tituba's companions, the accusations spread. Increasing numbers of women were accused, including some respected members of the church. Men too began to be named; the most prominent of these was the former minister of Salem Village, George Burroughs. The principal witnesses against the witches were a group of village females, ranging from preadolescents to mature women, who testified that the accused had afflicted them through supernatural means. Other neighbors came forward to support these accusations.

It was clearly necessary to go beyond the preliminary interrogations and to bring to trial those who had been accused. In June, a special court of Oyer and Terminer established by Governor Sir William Phips met in Salem Town. The first to be found guilty was Bridget Bishop, who was hanged on June 10. On July 19 five more were executed. Another five, including George Burroughs, were hanged on August 19. The last eight were executed on September 22. In addition to those who had died on the gallows, one man, Giles Cory, was crushed to death. Cory had refused to state whether he was guilty or innocent, and in accordance with established legal procedure, weights were placed on his body to force him to plead. At least two other accused witches died in prison.

But the trials were becoming an embarrassment to the colony. Even at the beginning there had been some concern expressed about the use of "spectral evidence": the testimony of witnesses that they had been harmed by the specter of a neighbor. After all, could not the Devil assume the shape of an innocent person? Increasingly, the clergy of the colony warned against over-reliance on this dubious form of evidence. And even if one overlooked the unsound nature of much of the case against the witches, it was apparent that the trials were not bringing the outbreak to an end. On the contrary, the chain of accusations was spreading well beyond Salem, and over 100 persons were ultimately suspected.

In the fall, Governor Phips disestablished the Court of Oyer and Terminer. The matter dragged on for some time in a superior court, but no more executions took place. Finally, in 1693, the Governor pardoned the remaining prisoners. It was now widely accepted that a tragic error had been made. January 15, 1697 was declared a day of fasting and prayer in Massachusetts, a time when the inhabitants asked for divine guidance. On that day one of the Salem judges, Samuel Sewall, publicly repented his part in the affair. The jurors who condemned the witches did the same.

Now came the task of explaining what had happened.

Background to Salem

New England was an offshoot of Europe, and to understand Salem in the seventeenth century it is necessary to know something of the history of the belief in witchery in the Old World. The outbreak of witch hunts in Massachusetts, in fact, came at the end of a particularly savage period of persecution of alleged witches in Europe, lasting roughly from the beginning of the sixteenth century to the end of the seventeenth. Prior to that time the execution of a witch was a relatively infrequent event. Although men believed in the reality of witchcraft, it was not regarded as a major social problem. But in the two centuries after 1500, the attack on suspected witches burst forth with extraordinary violence. By the thousands, persons accused of the crime were hunted down and executed.

The following essay by the popular nineteenth century American author, JOHN FISKE (1842–1901), is a brief survey of the phenomenon. Fiske attributes the start of the witch hunting of the sixteenth and seventeenth century to the work of an elite group—the "militant and unscrupulous" leaders of the Church. He also states that the growth of science finally ended the belief in witchcraft, "as clover chokes out weeds."

Fiske can be correctd on several points. First, executions of witches probably did not occur as frequently during the Middle Ages as he suggests. Second, Fiske is wrong in his assumption that the belief in witches was characteristic of all societies prior to the modern era. But more important than these specific corrections is the larger shift in historical scholarship that has occurred in recent years. This selection should thus be read as an example of the traditional interpretation of witchcraft; an interpretation that has now been seriously challenged.

1. A Traditional Interpretation of Witchcraft

In the year 1670 the provincial parliament of Normandy condemned a dozen women, young and old, to be burned at the stake. Their crime was attendance upon the Witches' Sabbath. An appeal was taken to the Crown, and Louis XIV was persuaded to spare their lives on condition that they should leave the kingdom and never return. Astonishment and indignation greeted this exercise of royal clemency, and the provincial parliament sent a petition to the king containing a grave remonstrance: "Your parliament have thought it their duty on occasion of these crimes, the greatest which men can

---

From John Fiske, *New France and New England* (Cambridge, Mass., 1902).

commit, to make you acquainted with the general and uniform feeling of the people of this province with regard to them; it being moreover a question in which are concerned the glory of God and the relief of your suffering subjects, who groan under their fears from the threats and menaces of this sort of persons. . . . We humbly supplicate your Majesty to reflect once more upon the extraordinary results which proceed from the malevolence of these people; on the loss of goods and chattels, and the deaths from unknown diseases, which are often the consequence of their menaces; . . . all of which may easily be proved to your Majesty's satisfaction by the records of various trials before your parliaments.'' It is pleasant to be able to add that Louis XIV was too well versed in the professional etiquette of royalty to withdraw a pardon which he had once granted, and so the poor women were saved from the flames. What we have especially to note is that the highest court of Normandy, representing the best legal knowledge of that province, in defining witchcraft as the infliction of disease or the destruction of property by unknown and mysterious means, describes it as the greatest of all crimes, and has no more doubt of its reality than of burglary or highway robbery.

This unquestioning belief in the reality of witchcraft has been shared by the whole human race, civilized and uncivilized alike, from prehistoric ages to the end of the seventeenth century. There are tribes of men with minds so little developed that travellers have doubted the existence of religious ideas among them; but none have been found so low as not to have some notion of witchcraft. Indeed, one of the most primitive and fundamental shapes which the relation of cause and effect takes in the savage mind is the assumed connection between disease or death and some malevolent personal agency. The conceptions of natural disease and natural death are attainable only by civilized minds. To the savage, who has scarcely an inkling of such a thing as laws of nature, all death is regarded as murder, either at the hands of a superhuman power that must be propitiated, or at the hands of some human being upon whom vengeance may be wreaked. The interpretation of disease is the same, and hence one of the chief occupations of medicine-men and priests among barbarous races is the detection and punishment of witches. Hence among all the superstitions,—or things that have ''stood over'' from primeval ages,—the belief in witchcraft has been the most deeply rooted and the most tenacious of life. In all times and places, until quite lately among the most advanced communities, the reality of witchcraft has been accepted without question, and scarcely any human belief is supported by so vast a quantity of recorded testimony.

At the present day, among communities like our own, we may observe a wonderful change. Among educated people the belief in witchcraft is practically extinct. It has not simply ceased to be taken seriously, but it has vanished from people's minds. . . .

What has caused this remarkable change in our mental attitude toward witchcraft? Surely not argument. Nobody has ever refuted the evidence that once seemed so conclusive in favor of the belief. For the most part we should now regard that evidence as not worth the trouble of refuting. Some powerful cause has made our minds insuperably inhospitable to such sort of evidence. That cause is the gigantic development of physical science since the days of Newton and Descartes. The minds of civilized people have become familiar with the conception of natural law, and that conception has simply stifled the old superstition as clover chokes out weeds. It has been observed that the existence of evidence in favour of witchcraft closely depends upon the disposition to believe it, so that when the latter ceases the former disappears. Accordingly we find no difficulty in understanding the universality of the belief until quite modern times. The disposition to believe was one of the oldest inheritances of the human mind, while the capacity for estimating evidence in cases of physical causation is one of its very latest and most laborious acquisitions.

In 1664 there was a witch trial at Bury St. Edmunds in Suffolk. The presiding justice was Sir Matthew Hale, one of the most eminent and learned of English judges. Two aged widows, Amy Duny and Rose Culender, were indicted for bewitching six young girls and one baby boy. This infant was seized with fainting turns, and his mother, suspecting witchcraft, took counsel of a country doctor, who told her to hang the child's crib blanket all day in the chimney corner, and if on taking it down at nightfall she should see anything strange there, she was not to be afraid of it, but to throw it into the fire. Well, when she was putting the baby to bed she took down the blanket, and a big toad fell out and hopped about the hearth. "Oh, put it in the fire, quick," said she to a boy present, who forthwith seized the poor toad with a pair of tongs and held it in the blaze. There was a flashing as of powder, and a strange noise, and then the toad vanished; but that same evening Amy Duny sitting by her own fireside had her face all smirched and scorched. Of course Amy was the toad, and it was natural that she should be vexed at such treatment, so that when the baby's sister suddenly sickened and died, and its mother grew lame enough to use crutches, it was all clearly due to Amy's diabolical arts. Absolute demonstration was reached when Amy was sentenced to death, for then her witch-power ceased, and the lame woman forthwith threw away her crutches and walked as briskly as anybody.

The other afflicted children complained of griping pains, and vomited crooked pins and twopenny nails. In the courtroom when Amy Duny or Rose Cullender came near to them, they threw their aprons over their heads and writhed in agony. It happened that among the magistrates present were some hard-headed Sadducees. Lord Cornwallis and Sir Edmund Bacon suspected these fits and torments of being a wicked sham. They blindfolded the girls, and had other old women approach and touch them. The girls went off into fits every time without discriminating between Rose or Amy and the other women. But this trifling flaw in the case was nothing when set off against the weighty evidence of a witness who declared that Rose Cullender had given him hard words, and shortly afterwards his hay-cart was stuck in passing through a gate. Another deposed that Amy Duny had said, "That chimney of yours will be falling down one of these days," and so sure enough it did. After this there could be no doubt in any reasonable mind that Rose had bewitched the cart and Amy the chimney. The learned justice in his charge aimed a rebuke at the scepticism exhibited by some of the magistrates; he declared that the reality of witchcraft was not open to question, since it was expressly affirmed in Holy Writ, and provided for in the criminal codes of all nations. The jury took less than half an hour to agree upon their verdict of guilty; and next week the two old dames were hanged at Cambridge, protesting their innocence with their last breath.

Upon just such so-called "evidence" more thousands of innocent persons than it will ever be possible to enumerate have been put to death under the forms of law. It is difficult to accept all the wholesale figures mentioned by old historians, yet the figures for which we have good authority are sufficiently dreadful. In general we may regard it as probable that during the Middle Ages executions for witchcraft occurred with much the same monotonous regularity as executions for murder and other felonies, but from time to time there were epidemics of terror when the number of victims was fearfully swelled. Now the famous bull of Pope Innocent VIII against witchcraft, published in 1484, marks the beginning of a new era in the history of the superstition. As literature and art have had their Golden Ages, so the sixteenth and seventeenth centuries were especially the Sulphurous Age of the witchcraft delusion. It was the period when the Church of Rome was engaged in a life and death struggle with heresy, and obnoxious persons suspected of heresy could sometimes be destroyed by a charge of witchcraft when there was no other method of reaching them. Thus the universal superstition was enlisted in the service of a militant and unscrupulous ecclesiastical organization with effects that were frightful. As it was understood that the diabolical crime of witchcraft was now to be stamped out once for all, the evidences of it were naturally found in plenty. The "Malleus Maleficarum," or Hammer of Witches, published in 1489, became the great text-book of the subject, and at no time since history began have the fires of hell been so often lighted upon earth as in the course of the next two centuries. . . .

Modern historians have begun to study witchcraft not as an end in itself, and not as an example of the struggle between superstition and science, but rather as a clue to the way common people of centuries past viewed the world they lived in. The following review essay by LAWRENCE STONE (b. 1919) addresses a broad range of subjects such as the tensions of village life, the spread of poverty, and the social position of women. He is also interested in how societies change with time; and he speculates on why witch-beliefs eventually lost their hold on the European mind—and why these beliefs are reviving in our own era. Stone's message is clear: witchcraft cannot be studied in isolation from the larger framework of the social, economic, and intellectual history of the West. His is a view that is far more complex than the one given by Fiske in the preceding selection.

Lawrence Stone is a professor of history at Princeton. This essay originally appeared as a review of several recent books on witchcraft and magic, including Witchcraft at Salem *by Chadwick Hansen,* Witchcraft in Tudor and Stuart England *by Alan MacFarlane,* Magistrates et Sorciers en France au 17ᵉ Siècle *by Robert Mandrou, and* Religion and the Decline of Magic *by Keith Thomas.*

2. A New Interpretation of Witchcraft

Until the last few years the study of witchcraft has been almost entirely left either to unscholarly cranks or to indignant rationalists, the latter more concerned to castigate the witch-baiters for their credulity and cruelty than to understand what the phenomonen was all about. Mr. MacFarlane's study of witchcraft in Essex, illuminated by detailed knowledge of the findings of modern anthropology, the reassessment of the witchcraft outbreak of 1692 in Salem by Professor Hansen, drawing on the findings of abnormal psychology, the examination of the change in attitude of the French magistrates by Pro-

---

From Lawrence Stone, "The Disenchantment of the World," *The New York Review of Books,* (December 12, 1971), pp. 17–25. Reprinted with permission from *The New York Review of Books.* Copyright © 1971 Nyrev, Inc.

fessor Mandrou, and Mr. Thomas's major survey of the climate of opinion in England on all kinds of magical beliefs—these books at last make it possible to answer some of the basic questions. Moreover by a happy chance they complement one another, since each approaches the problem from a different angle. From the findings of all four, a composite picture can be drawn which has the appearance of plausibility.

Belief in witchcraft reached a higher level of consciousness in the sixteenth century than it had in the Middle Ages. The first reason for this was the enormous increase in belief in the powers of the Devil brought about by the Reformation. The early Protestants indignantly rejected all claims that God could be persuaded or cajoled into interfering for the good in the workings of nature, but at the same time they strengthened claims that the Devil was responsible for all the forces of evil in the world. Thus they rejected white magic for the Church, while offering an official explanation for black magic. This paradoxical development arose since an immanent Devil was the necessary and logical complement to an immanent God. While the latter ruled in heaven, the former became, in John Knox's words, "the Prince and God of the World." Belief in the supernatural forces of evil abroad in the world was thus reinforced by Protestant doctrine, which soon also spilled over into Counter-Reformation beliefs.

Secondly the Reformation theologians abandoned the only approved remedies against the machinations of the Devil, namely exorcism, holy relics, and the sprinkling of holy water, thus removing the official means of cure at a time when the disease was officially said to be spreading.

Third, the pressure of social and economic change was breaking down the old values of the intimate, "face-to-face" peasant communities and creating great tension in the villages. In particular, poverty was becoming too widespread to be handled on a voluntary basis, and the moral duty of the rich to give alms to the poor and the moral right of the poor to demand them were both being called into question. As a result of this breakdown there was constant friction between increasingly reluctant alms givers and increasingly exigent poor old women. The former had residual feelings of guilt at the decline of their charitable impulses and felt resentful toward those who badgered them. If the guilty refuser of charity then sufered a misfortune, he immediately suspected that the rejected alms seeker had bewitched him. This transferred his guilt back to the alms seeker and diverted the frustrations felt against the whole system of poor relief on to the persecution of an individual. The psychological mechanism of witch persecution is now clear enough.

Fourth, continental Europe, although to a much lesser extent than England, saw the acceptance among the educated of a comprehensive conspiracy theory, an invention of obsessed priests and intellectuals. This was the notion of a widespread secret society of witches, assembling in covens, making pacts with the Devil, and copulating with him at Sabbats, to which they traveled on broomsticks. Evidence for this extraordinary farrago of nonsense was soon provided by a flood of confessions, either the product of autosuggestion in hysterics or extracted by the use of the most terrible torture, the increased use of which was the last contributory cause. As we have found out again in the twentieth century, the torturer can obtain detailed evidence of the most absurd conspiracies and the most unlikely conspirators, provided he is told what and whom to find, for in their torment the subjects will freely confess to anything and will accuse any or everyone they know.

It is to the credit of the English that the common law legal system greatly inhibited, if it did not altogether prevent, the use of "the unEnglish method of torture." As a result, the destructive potentialities of the witch hunting craze were never allowed to develop to the degree that they did on the continent and in Scotland. Although prosecution was extremely common in England, the death penalty was relatively rare, owing to the care with which the magistrates and clergy normally approached the problem of obtaining satisfactory evidence.

Fear of evil spirits manipulated by witchcraft thus spread in the sixteenth century in a society which believed implicitly that any inexplicable event was caused by magic, in which the Church had abandoned its old miracle-working weapons, and in which the powers of the Devil were thought to have greatly increased. It was also a society undergoing great social stress, in which the moral duty of the rich toward the poor was no longer clear, and in which the only resort of the poor against injustice was the invocation of black magic. It is clear that village communities must have spent an enormous amount of time discussing suspicions of witchcraft and ways of dealing with it. The prosecutions were only the top of the iceberg, and below the surface there was a constant warfare in progress between white and black magic. Only if black magic seemed to be unstoppable by other means was there recourse to the courts.

So far, we have treated witchcraft exclusively as part of a system of beliefs whose function was to alleviate anxiety caused by ignorance of causation and incapacity to control the environment. It may also have served a latent function as well, as a restraint upon social conflict. Everything we know about village life, especially in the sixteenth and seventeenth centuries, suggests that it was bad-tempered, quarrelsome, and riddled with hatreds, jealousies, and feelings of guilt. Fear of being bewitched must have acted as a powerful incentive to the financially secure in the prime of life to be kind and generous to the old, the sick, and the poor. Conversely, fear of being accused of witchcraft must have been a powerful incentive to the latter to be amiable and courteous to the former.

On the other hand witchcraft allegations deflected aggressive impulses and social tensions away from the maladjusted institutions and conventions that lay at the root of the trouble. In this particular case the root was the economic system which made the poor so demanding and burdensome and the rich so guilty and resentful, and the status system which left women without a meaningful social position. Witchcraft beliefs therefore postponed the necessary institutional and intellectual changes by allowing society to deflect its rage onto the persecution of a scapegoat. As a result these dysfunctional institutions were allowed to struggle on instead of being rapidly transformed.

Those who launched accusations of witchcraft can be seen to fall into three categories. The first, and by far the most common, were simple village peasants who had committed some breach of the social conventions in their behavior toward the accused—usually it was the refusal to give alms or lend money. The accused had consequently let fall some expression of malice—usually a curse—and the accuser had subsequently been struck by misfortune. The sufferer first made application to a "cunning man," who helped him to confirm his suspicions of the identity of the witch who was the cause of his troubles. Because of this relationship between the accuser and the accused, the former almost always enjoyed a higher social and economic status than the latter.

The second class of accuser was the hysteric, usually a woman, who went into severe fits and spoke with voices, accusing all and sundry of bewitching her. In some of the most sensational cases, it is clear that the predominant role was played by a local epidemic of hysteria, superimposed on a general belief in magic. Hysteria is extremely catching, and as a result from time to time, as in Salem in 1692, or in some French nunneries, whole communities would be shattered by an epidemic of witchcraft hysteria which could well engulf the accused as well as the accusers, and could temporarily blind the authorities to the flimsy nature of the evidence. . . .

The third and rarest class of accuser was the dedicated ideological witch-finder, armed with the *Malleus Maleficarum* or some similar inquisitorial handbook, who roamed about the countryside terrorizing whole neighborhoods. A fearful example of the havoc wrought in a suggestible population by these men was the mass prosecution of fifty witches in the Manningtree area of Essex in 1645, which was launched by two witch-finders. Because of the presence on the scene of these professionals, this is one of the rare cases in England in which the confessions made mention of those stock European practices of assembling in covens, copulating with the Devil, kissing his arse, etc.

On the other hand it is clear that these professional witch-finders with their obvious anal-erotic obsessions were only exploiting and encouraging pre-existing fears and hatreds and delusions within the village community. Indeed, the whole history of witchcraft has been distorted by concentration upon these rare but highly sensational cases, heavily spiced with sex and sadism, which were launched by hysterical women or by professional witch-finders. What has been ignored is the regular flow of complaints and prosecutions from ordinary persons who had suffered inexplicable misfortune.

Those accused of witchcraft can also be fitted into three categories, although the distinctions are by no means as sharp as they are between the types of accuser, and the risk of over-schematization is greater. The first group are the genuine witches, resentful persons of low social status and economic level, who tried to take revenge upon their neighbors, usually for some real injury. By the use of spells, rituals, potions, the sticking of pins into waxen dolls, etc., they seriously tried to induce sickness or death in human beings or cattle. Witchcraft was the weapon of the weak against the strong for, apart from scolding and arson, it was the only weapon they had.

Magic, of which witchcraft is a part, only works to the extent that people think it works, for its effects are dependent on the psychosomatic power of belief and not on physical properties. Since society believed in witchcraft, the victims were often suggestible enough to be severely affected by it. There is therefore a good deal to be said for the view of skeptics like Hobbes, who denied the capacity of witchcraft to do any concrete harm but thought that witches should be punished for the malice of their intentions.

The second category of the accused was the innocent, who undoubtedly formed the great majority. Some of them denied their guilt to the end, but very many were browbeaten, tortured, or confused by the strength of popular opinion among their neighbors and by the pressure of prolonged interrogation into confessing crimes of which they were not guilty. The third category were the hysterics, often women or pubescent children, who gave free rein in their voluntary confessions to auto-suggestive fantasies about affectionate dealings with animal familiars or loveless copulations with the Devil.

It is very noticeable that during the peak period of witchcraft activity and persecution in the West, most of the black witches were women, and most of the white witches and the accusers were men. Unfortunately, anthropologists have so far been unable satisfactorily to identify and isolate the causes why in some African societies today the black witches are nearly all women, in others they are nearly all men, and in others again they are mixed. Theories about the economic predominance of women in Ghana or about generational conflict in Massachusetts simply do not apply to other societies.

In this vacuum of scientific theory, the historian can only speculate in the void. Is it possible that the practice of witchcraft was one of the very few ways in which a woman could impress herself on a male chauvinist world, at a time when economic opportunities were limited, the structure of the family was changing only very slowly, and when feminine eroticism was strongly condemned? Is it possible that the decline of witchcraft was brought about to some extent by a partial adaptation of the family in order to give women a greater share of respect, authority, and sexual satisfaction? Is it more than coincidence that witches vanish just at the time when Fanny Hill appears?

If so, then the rise and fall of witchcraft in the West has to be associated with different stages of a revolution of rising female expectations, generated in turn by the growth of literacy and the rise of individualism that were accidental by-products of the Reformation. All this is very fanciful, but the sexual element in witchcraft in the West is too obvious to be ignored. . . .

* * *

Why did the persecution of witches decline in the seventeenth century? What is absolutely certain is that the lead was taken by the lay and clerical elite, who were the first to lose faith in the system of beliefs upon which the persecutions were founded. Belief in the efficacy of magic, and therefore of the reality of black witchcraft, survived in the general population until recent times. Indeed there are sound reasons for doubting whether belief in magic has ever died out in the West.

Today, at the apogee of our scientific, rationalist, technological civilization, magical beliefs are spreading once more. Millions of lucky charms hang in cars to ward off traffic accidents; astrological advice is regularly published in the popular newspapers, and courses on the subject are just beginning to appear at the universities in response to student demand; the casting of horoscopes, often assisted by computers, is a booming growth industry; every year huge crowds of the sick pour into Lourdes in the hope of a miraculous cure.

Perhaps most disturbing of all is the current faddish revival of interest in witchcraft, evidence for which is provided by the spate of new historical works, reprints of inquisitorial handbooks and of reports of notorious witch trials, imaginative re-creations of historical events by talented novelists like François Mallet-Joris and fashionable film directors like Ken Russell, and the beginning of semiserious organized witch cults in California.

The problem, therefore, is how to explain a change in attitude in the seventeenth century not so much among the peasantry who launched the prosecutions as among the elite who controlled the legal process, the clergy and the magistrates. The great strength of Mr. Thomas's book is his insistence that the change cannot be considered in isolation, as hitherto it has been, but must be looked at in the light of magical beliefs of all kinds. There is a basic intellectual and practical unity between magic, astrology, and witchcraft. William Lilly, for example, practiced astrology, medicine, spirit-raising, treasure hunting, and the conjuration of fairies. Astrologers and their rivals, the cunning men, were often called in to diagnose cases of witchcraft.

The question must therefore be broadened, and we must ask not what was the cause of the decline in the belief in witchcraft in the seventeenth century, but what was the cause of the decline in the belief in magic. One possibility is the growth of mechanical philosophy. The trouble with this explanation is that skepticism about magic and witchcraft was growing among clergy, lawyers, doctors, and lay magistrates in the early seventeenth century, before the new natural science had made any real impact. In any case, magical overtones pervaded early seventeenth-century science. Hermetic thought was a stimulus to heliocentric theories, belief in the magical properties of numbers to mathematics, astrology to astronomy. The discovery of magnetism actually increased belief in the spirits, since it seemed to prove that physical objects could influence one another from a distance.

More important than any scientific discoveries was the change in scientific attitudes, namely the new Baconian demand for experimental proof. The idea that "there is no certain knowledge without demonstration" slowly eroded belief in all kinds of magical explanations for events, just at the time when the lawyers were tightening up their rules of evidence in a parallel demand for more rigorous proof. But this rational approach to evidence could not develop in a world of arbitrary magic. A prior condition for the emergence of the spirit of scientific inquiry was therefore the development of religious belief in an orderly universe in which God's providence operates according to natural laws.

Organized and established religion must be seen as a system of explanation and recourse parallel to and rivaling those of magic and astrology. Hobbes rightly pointed out that the distinction between superstition and religion is in the eye of the beholder. "This fear of things invisible is the natural seed of that which everyone in himself calleth Religion; and in them that worship or fear that power otherwise than they do, superstition." Although religion deals with fundamentals, and magic with particulars, ministers and witch doctors were clearly rival practitioners in the application of supernatural powers to the problems and miseries of this world. Both tended to blame individuals—the former the sufferer for his sin, the latter the malicious manipulator of spirits.

Presbyterians and astrologers offered alternative systems of predestination. Professor Evans-Pritchard has recently suggested that "when religious beliefs, whether those of spiritual cults or ancestor cults, are strong, witchcraft beliefs are relatively weak." As we have seen, the distinction between religion and magic was hopelessly blurred in the Middle Ages, and the first stage in making a separation occurred when the Protestant reformers rejected all claims to miracle-working powers for their churches. The second important step, however, was taken at the end of the seventeenth century; when religion became more rational and God's providence was at last regarded as working in strict conformity to natural laws. It was the natural theology of the eighteenth century which finally broke the habit of ascribing misfortune to moral delinquency or malevolent agency.

Another of Hobbes's theories was that "in these four things, opinion of ghosts, ignorance of second causes, devotion to which men fear, and taking of things casual for prognostics, consisteth the natural seed of religion, which by reason of the different fancies, judgements, and passions of several men, hath grown up into ceremonies so different, that those which are used by one man are for the most part ridiculous to another." It is undoubtedly true that both magic and the various Christian churches and sects all offer explanations to fill the gaps caused by human ignorance of causation, but their scope is not purely determined by the ignorance. If this were so, neither would have shrunk until technological control of nature had increased, but the chronology, as we have seen, is wrong.

At the beginning of the seventeenth century Bacon had defined the aims of the new science:

> The end of our foundation is the knowledge of causes and the secret motion of things, and the enlarging of the bounds of human empire, to the effecting of all things possible.

This was indeed the goal, but during the critical period when magic was in decline and the magical properties of religion also in retreat in the face of natural theology, there was really no great technological breakthrough. Doctors were just about as powerless to cure disease or to prolong life in 1700 as they were in 1500, the means of recovery of stolen property were as inadequate as ever, forecasting the future was as unreliable as ever.

What had changed, however, was man's aspirations and expectations. There was now a belief abroad that the human condition could be improved, partly by social action such as founding hospitals or legislating poor relief, and partly by making technological discoveries. There was also a new willingness to tolerate ignorance, instead of filling the hitherto intolerable void with assumptions about the intervention of demons or angels, or the direct providence of God.

What undermined educated belief in magic, and with it educated belief in witchcraft, was thus not the success of technology in reducing the area of ignorance. It was rather a new religious attitude of self-help, an acceptance of the doctrine that God helps those who help themselves, and that supernatural intervention in the workings of nature was now so rare as to be negligible for all practical purposes. Such are the broad conclusions of Mr. Thomas's important book, parts of which are supported by the works of Professors MacFarlane, Mandrou, and Hansen. . . .

* * *

We can now see, perhaps for the first time, the complex chronological interaction of magic, religion, and science as rival explanatory systems. The early Reformation renounced the magical powers of religion, and unofficial magic presumably poured in to fill the void. In its official doctrine, however, the reformers greatly stimulated belief in the Devil as the instigator of all misfortune and evil, and of Antichrist as the embodiment of evil on earth, who had to be destroyed before the reign of Jesus could begin. It was only much later on, after a century of turmoil and bloody persecution, that the profounder aspects of the new religion came to the fore. By the late seventeenth century Protestantism's more rational and coherent view of nature and its relationship of God's providence had at last produced a state of mind to which magical or miraculous explanations of events were unacceptable. Later still, this religious-inspired rationalism began to undermine religion itself.

The relation of magic and science went through the same two stages of symbiosis and antagonism. For a century, magic went hand in hand with science, but eventually science broke away and destroyed its partner's credibility, at any rate among the educated classes. Much later still, in the nineteenth century, it also broke with religion, which it began to destroy too.

This is not a simple story of heroes and devils, of reason battling unreason, nor is it enough to treat it as one of the more bizarre aspects of human folly. The most deeply held beliefs of the past seem wholly irrational to us, as no doubt many of our own will seem to posterity. When all is said, however, the abiding distinction of the West has been that in the last three hundred years it has gone further than any other society the world has ever known to rid itself of these ancient fears and superstitions. The process is perhaps the most important intellectual change since man emerged from caves. But in the light of the current revival of belief in magic and the irrational, neither arrogance nor complacency is in order when one views the long, messy, continuing struggle which has slowly led to what Max Weber described as "the disenchantment of the world."

As a result of this struggle modern man now walks upon a knife edge. On the one side is a "technetronic" society, smooth, impersonal, rational, and scientific, a kind of universal IBM company ruled over by the computer. While it can be supremely efficient, it is also drab and sterile, leaving no place either for the emotions, including the finer ones of love and compassion, or for the sense of aesthetic mystery and wonder which is at the root of all great literature, art, and music. On the other side is a society at the mercy of prejudice and passion, driven forward by wholly irrational beliefs which stunt the mind and prevent effective action for human betterment. While it may be warm and vibrant, it is also full of cruelty, hate, and fear. The naked ape had better watch his step.

The Verdict of Contemporaries

To the majority of orthodox Puritans at the onset of the Salem trials, the outbreaks of witchcraft were just what they appeared to be: a certain number of wicked persons were in league with the Devil and had supernatural powers to afflict their innocent neighbors. But there were some in Massachusetts who had their doubts, and their numbers increased as the trials progressed. They were disturbed by the flimsy nature of the evidence and by the spread of accusations in ever-widening circles. It was inevitable that COTTON MATHER (1663–1728) should be drawn into this controversy. The third-generation Puritan minister had established himself as an authority on witchcraft when, in 1689, he published Memorable Providences Relating to Witchcrafts and Possessions. *Now, three years later, the governor of the colony asked him to speak in defense of the Salem trials.*

The result was The Wonders of the Invisible World, *published in late 1692. The twenty-nine-year old author took pains to state, "I Report matters not as an Advocate but as an Historian." It is possible to take Mather at his word and to regard* The Wonders of the Invisible World *as the first historical interpretation of Salem. The thesis is simple: the sentences of death were fully deserved because the witches were guilty. It was no accident, said Mather, that the outbreak had occurred at Salem, "the Center, and after a sort, the First-born of our English Settlements." New England had been a land ruled by the Devil until the Puritans had arrived to establish a holy commonwealth. Now the Devil was launching a counterattack to regain his dominion, and because the people of New England had fallen away from the piety of their ancestors, this invasion had come close to succeeding. Indeed, those who doubted the wisdom of the magistrates were themselves contributing to the Devil's cause. By repentence and unity, however, Satan could be defeated.*

To prove that the case against the witches was overwhelming, and that "spectral evidence" provided by witnesses was reliable, Mather described in detail the proceedings against several of the accused. Included in the following excerpt is his account of the case against Bridget Bishop, the first witch to be hung at Salem.

3. Satan's Attack on New England

The New-Englanders are a People of God settled in those which were once the Devil's Teritories; and it may easily be supposed that the Devil was

---

From Cotton Mather, *The Wonders of the Invisible World* (London, 1862).

exceedingly disturbed when he perceived such a People here accomplishing the Promise of old made unto our Blessed Jesus, That He should have the Utmost Parts of the Earth for his Possession. There was not a greater Uproar among the Ephesians when the Gospel was first brought among them than there was among The Powers of the Air (after whom those Ephesians walked) when first the Silver Trumpets of the Gospel here made the Joyful Sound. The Devil, thus Irritated, immediately try'd all sorts of Methods to overturn this poor Plantation: and so much of the Church as was Fled into this Wilderness, immediately found The Serpent cast out of his Mouth a Flood for the carrying of it away. I believe that never were more Satanical Devices used for the Unsetling of any People under the Sun, than what have been Employ'd for the Extirpation of the Vine which God has here Planted. . . .

But, All those Attempts of Hell have hitherto been Abortive, many an Ebenezer [i.e., prayer] has been Erected unto the Praise of God by his Poor People here and Having obtained Help from God, we continue to this Day. Wherefore the Devil is now making one Attempt more upon us; an Attempt more Difficult, more Surprizing, more snarl'd with unintelligible Circumstances than any that we have hitherto Encountered; an Attempt so Critical that if we get well through, we shall soon enjoy Halcyon Days with all the Vultures of Hell Trodden under our Feet. He has wanted his Incarnate Legions to Persecute us, as the People of God have in the other Hemisphere been Persecuted: he has therefore drawn forth his more Spiritual ones to make an Attacque upon us. We have been advised by some Credible Christians yet alive that a Malefactor, accused of Witchcraft as well as Murder, and Executed in this place more than Forty Years ago, did then give Notice of An Horrible Plot against the Country by Witchcraft, and a Foundation of Witchcraft, then laid, which if it were not seasonably discovered would probably Blow up, and pull down all the Churches in the Country. And we have now with Horror seen the Discovery of such a Witchcraft! An Army of Devils is horribly broke in upon the place which is the Center, and after a sort, the First-born of our English Settlements: and the Houses of the Good People there are fill'd with the doleful Shrieks of their Children and Servants, Tormented by Invisible Hands, with Tortures altogether preternatural. After the Mischiefs there Endeavoured, and since in part Conqured, the terrible Plague of Evil Angels hath made its Progress into some other places, where other Persons have been in like manner Diabolically handled. These our poor Afflicted Neighbors quickly after they become Infected and Infested with these Demons, arrive to a Capacity of Discerning those which they conceive the Shapes of their Troublers; and notwithstanding the Great and Just Suspicion that the Demons might Impose the Shapes of Innocent Persons in their

Spectral Exhibitions upon the Sufferers, (which may perhaps prove no small part of the Witch-Plot in the issue) yet many of the Persons thus Represented, being Examined, several of them have been Convicted of a very Damnable Witchcraft: yea, more than One Twenty have Confessed that they have signed unto a Book which the Devil show'd them, and Engaged in his Hellish Design of Bewitching and Ruining our Land. We know not, at least *I* know not, how far the Delusions of Satan may be Interwoven into some Circumstances of the Confessions; but one would think all the Rules of Understanding Humane Affairs are at an end, if after so many most Voluntary Harmonious Confessions, made by Intelligent Persons of all Ages, in sundry Towns, at Several Times, we must not Believe the main strokes wherein those Confessions all agree: especially when we have a thousand preternatural Things every day before our eyes, wherein the Confessors do acknowledge their Concernment [i.e., involvement], and give Demonstration of their being so Concerned. If the Devils now can strike the minds of men with any Poisons of so fine a Composition and Operation, that Scores of Innocent People shall Unite in Confessions of a Crime, which we see actually committed, it is a thing prodigious, beyond the Wonders of the former Ages, and it threatens no less than a sort of Dissolution upon the World. Now, by these Confessions 'tis Agreed That the Devil has made a dreadful knot of Witches in the Country, and by the help of Witches has dreadfully increased that Knot: That these Witches have driven a Trade of Commisioning their Confederate Spirits to do all sorts of Mischiefs to the Neighbours, whereupon there have ensured such Mischievous consequences upon the Bodies and Estates of the Neighborhood, as could not otherwise be accounted for: yea, That at prodigious Witch-Meetings the Wretches have proceeded so far as to Concert and Consult the Methods of Rooting out the Christian Religion from this Country, and setting up instead of it, perhaps a more gross Diabolism than ever the World saw before. . . .

But that which most of all Threatens us in our present Circumstances is the Misunderstanding, and so the Animosity, whereinto the Witchcraft now Raging has Enchanted us. The Embroiling, first of our Spirits and then of our Affairs is evidently as considerable a Branch of the Hellish Intrigue which now vexes us as any one Thing whatsoever. The Devil has made us like a Troubled Sea, and the Mire and Mud begins now also to heave up apace. Even Good and Wise Men suffer themselves to fall into their Paroxysms; and the Snake which the Devil is now giving us fetches up the Dirt which before lay still at the bottom of our sinful Hearts. If we allow the Mad Dogs of Hell to poyson us by biting us, we shall imagine that we see nothing but such things about us, and like such things, fly upon all that we see. Were it not for what is in us, for my part I should not fear a thousand Legions of Devils: 'tis by our Quarrels that we spoil our Prayers; and if our humble zealous, and united Prayers are once hindered: Alas, the Philistines of Hell have cut our Locks for us; they will then blind us, mock us, ruine us. . . .

The Tryal of Bridget Bishop, alias Oliver, At the Court of Oyer and Terminer Held at Salem, June 2, 1692

She was indicted for Bewitching of several Persons in the Neighbourhood, the Indictment being drawn up according to the Form in such Cases usual. And pleading Not Guilty, there were brought in several persons who had long undergone many kinds of Miseries, which were preternaturally inflicted, and generally ascribed unto an horrible Witchcraft. There was little occasion to prove the Witchcraft, it being evident and notorious to all beholders. Now to fix Witchcraft on the Prisoner at the Bar, the first thing used was the Testimony of the Bewitched; whereof several testifi'd That the Shape of the Prisoner did oftentimes very grievously Pinch them, Choak them, Bite them, and Afflict them; urging them to write their Names in a Book, which the said Spectre called Ours. One of them did further testifie that it was the Shape of this Prisoner, with another, which one day took her from her Wheel, and carrying her to the Riverside, threatend there to Drown her if she did not Sign to the Book mentioned: which yet she refused. Others of them did also testifie that the said Shape did in her Threats brag to them that she had been the Death of sundry Persons, then by her named; and that she had Ridden a Man then likewise named. Another testifi'd, the Apparition of Ghosts unto the Spectre of Bishop, crying out, you Murdered us! About the truth whereof, there was in the Matter of Fact but far too much suspicion.

It was testifi'd, That at the Examination of the Prisoner before the Magistrates, the Bewitched were extreamly tortured. If she did but cast her Eyes on them, they were presently struck down; and this in such a manner as there could be no Collusion in the Business. But upon the Touch of her Hand upon them when they lay in their Swoons, they would immediately Revive; and not upon the Touch of any one else. Moreover, Upon some Special Actions of her Body, as the shaking of her Head, or the turning of her Eyes, they presently and painfully fell into the like postures. And many of the like Accidents now fell out, while she was at the Bar. . . .

One Deliverance Hobbs, who had confessed being a Witch, was now tormented by the Spectres for her Confession. And she now testifi'd That this Bishop tempted her to sign the Book again, and to deny what she had confess'd. She affirm'd That it was the Shape of this Prisoner which whipped her with Iron Rods, to compel her thereunto. And she affirmed that this Bishop was at a General Meeting of the Witches in a Field at Salem-Village, and there partook of a Diabolical Sacrament in Bread and Wine then administered. . . .

Samuel Shattock testify'd That in the Year 1680, this Bridget Bishop often came to his House upon such frivolous and foolish Errands that they suspected she came indeed with a purpose of mischief. Presently whereupon his eldest Child, which was of as promising Health and Sense as any Child of its Age, began to droop exceedingly; and the oftner that Bishop came to the House, the worse grew the Child. As the Child would be standing at the Door, he would be thrown and bruised against the Stones by an invisible Hand, and in like sort knock his Face against the sides of the House, and bruise it after a miserable manner. . . .

To crown all, John Bly and William Bly testify'd That being employ'd by Bridget Bishop to help to take down the Cellar-wall of the old house wherein she formerly lived, they did in holes of the said old Wall find several Poppets [i.e., dolls], made of Rags and Hogs-bristles, with headless Pins in them, the Points being outward; whereof she could give no account unto the Court that was reasonable or tolerable. . . .

One thing that made against the Prisoner was her being evidently convicted of gross Lying in the court, several times, while she was making her plea; but besides this, a Jury of Women found a preternatural Teat upon her Body: But upon a second search, within 3 or 4 hours, there was no such thing to be seen.* There was also an Account of other People whom this Woman had Afflicted; and there might have been many more, if they had been enquired for; but there was no need of them.

There was one very strange thing more, with which the Court was newly entertained. As this Woman was under a Guard, passing by the great and spacious Meeting-house of Salem, she gave a look towards the House: And immediately a Demon invisibly entring the Meeting-house, tore down a part of it, so that tho' there was no Person to be seen there, yet the People, at the noise, running in, found a Board, which was strongly fastend with several Nails, transported unto another quarter of the House.

**Editor's note*: When an unusual mark or growth was found on the body of an alleged witch, it was usually assumed that this was a teat provided by the Devil to enable the witch to nurse a demon. The fact that such a "preternatural teat" seemed to appear and disappear on the body of Bridget Bishop is used as evidence by Mather to prove that she was guilty of witchcraft.

The Wonders of the Invisible World failed to convince Cotton Mather's countrymen. The same governor who had urged him to write a defense of the trials later dissolved the Court of Oyer and Terminer and pardoned those who remained in prison. Mather had hoped that the people of New England would repent their scepticism; what they repented instead was their part in the tragedy of Salem. And in the course of this change in opinion, Mather himself came under attack. In 1697 the Boston merchant ROBERT CALEF (1648–1719) wrote a vitriolic denunciation of the trials and of Cotton Mather's role. This book was published in London in 1700 with the sarcastic title More Wonders of the Invisible World. *Not surprisingly, Cotton Mather angrily described* More Wonders *as a libelous book, and called its author a "sort of Saducee . . . who makes little Conscience of lying."*

*These two books—*The Wonders *and* More Wonders*—represent the polarized attitudes towards witchcraft of seventeenth century New Englanders. To Mather the trials were a timely and proper exercise of authority against a monstrous evil; to Calef the trials themselves constituted the evil. In the centuries since Salem it has been Calef's view that has prevailed.*

4. An Attack on the Trials

In a time when not only England in particular, but almost all Europe had been labouring against the Usurpations of Tyranny and Slavery, The English America has not been behind in a share in the Common calamities; more especially New-England has met not only with such calamities as are common to the rest, but with several aggravations enhansing such Afflictions, by the Devastations and Cruelties of the Barbarous Indians in their Eastern borders, etc.

But this is not all, they have been harrast (on many accounts) by a more dreadful Enemy, as will herein appear to the considerate.

[In the following three paragraphs, Calef summarizes Cotton Mather's version of the witchcraft epidode. The number at the beginning of each paragraph refers to the corresponding page number in the 1692 edition of Mather's *The Wonders of the Invisible World*.]

P. 66.   Were it as we are told in *Wonders of the Invisible World*, that the Devils were walking about our Streets with lengthened Chains making a dreadful noise in our Ears, and Brimstone, even without a Metaphor, was making a horrid and a hellish stench in our Nostrils,

---

From Robert Calef, *More Wonders of the Invisible World*, reprinted in *Narratives of the Witchcraft Cases*, edited by G. L. Burr (New York, 1914), pp. 289–393.

P. 49.   And that the Devil exhibiting himself ordinarily as a black-Man, had decoy'd a fearful knot of Proud, Froward, Ignorant, Envious and Malitious Creatures, to list themselves in his horrid Service, by entring their Names in a Book tendered unto them; and that they have had their Meetings and Sacraments, and associated themselves to destroy the Kingdom of our Lord Jesus Christ, in these parts of the World; having each of them their Spectres, or Devils Commissionated by them, and representing of them, to be the Engines of their Malice, by these wicked Spectres siezing poor People about the Country with various and bloody Torments. And of those evidently preternatural Torments some to[o] have died. And that they have bewitched some even so far, a to make them self destroyers, and others in many Towns here and there languish'd under their evil hands. The people thus afflicted miserably scratch'd and bitten; and that the same Invisible Furies did stick Pins in them, and scald them, distort and disjoint them, with a Thousand other Plagues; and sometimes drag them out of their Chambers, and carry them over Trees and Hills Miles together, many of them being tempted to sign the Devils Laws.

P. 7[0].   Those furies whereof several have killed more People perhaps than would serve to make a Village.

If this be the true state of the Afflictions of this Country, it is very deplorable, and beyond all other outward Calamities miserable. But if on the other side, the Matter be as others do understand it, That the Devil has been too hard for us by his Temptations, signs, and lying Wonders, with the help of pernicious notions, formerly imbibed and professed; together with the Accusations of a parcel of possessed, distracted, or lying Wenches, accusing their Innocent Neighbours, pretending they see their Spectres (i.e.) Devils in their likeness Afflicting of them, and that God in righteous Judgment (after Men had ascribed his Power to Witches, of Commissionating Devils to do these things) may have given them over to strong delusions to believe lyes, etc. And to let loose the Devils of Envy, Hatred, Pride, Cruelty, and Malice against each other; yet still disguised under the Mask of Zeal for God, and left them to the branding one another with the odious Name of Witch; and upon the Accusation of those above mentioned, Brother to Accuse and Prosecute Brother, Children their Parents, Pastors and Teachers their immediate Flock unto death; Shepherds becoming Wolves, Wise Men Infatuated; People hauled to Prisons, with a bloody noise pursuing to, and insulting over, the (true) Sufferers at Execution, while some are fleeing from that call'd Justice, Justice it self fleeing before such Accusations, when once it did but begin to refrain further proceedings, and to question such Practices, some making their Escape out of Prisons, rather than by an obstinate Defence of their

Innocency, to run so apparent hazard of their Lives; Estates seized, Families of Children and others left to the Mercy of the Wilderness (not to mention here the Numbers proscribed, dead in Prisons, or Executed, etc.)

All which Tragedies, tho begun in one Town, or rather by one Parish, has Plague-like spread more than through that Country. And by its Eccho giving a brand of Infamy to this whole Country throughout the World,

If this were the Miserable case of this Country in the time thereof, and that the Devil had so far prevailed upon us in our Sentiments and Actions, as to draw us from so much as looking into the Scriptures for our guidance in these pretended Intricacies, leading us to a trusting in blind guides, such as the corrupt practices of some other Countries, or the bloody Experiments of Bodin,* and such other Authors—Then tho our Case be most miserable, yet it must be said of New-England, Thou hast destroyed thy self, and brought this greatest of Miseries upon thee.

Editor's note: Jean Bodin (1529–1596) was a French writer and jurist notorious for his persecution of witches.

"I have special reasons moving me to bear my testimony," said the REV. JOHN HALE (1636–1700) in his book A Modest Inquiry into the Nature of Witchcraft. *Hale, the minister of Beverly, Massachusetts, was a participant in the Salem episode, and he had actively supported the work of the magistrates. But ironically, his own wife was accused of witchcraft in the fall of 1692, and Hale became convinced that the trials had been a ghastly mistake. Writing five years later, Hale tried to draw lessons from the tragedy. The historian Perry Miller (see selection 12) describes* A Modest Inquiry *as a "sad, troubled, and honest book," and one can see in it the tortured effort of a devout man who, lacking the arrogance of Mather or the anger of Calef, tried to arrive at the truth. Although the book was completed in 1697, it was not published until 1702—two years after the author's death. It is likely that this was Hale's wish.*

5. The Lessons of Salem

The Holy Scriptures inform us that the Doctrine of Godliness is a great Mystery, containing the Mysteries of the Kingdom of Heaven: Mysteries which require great search for the finding out: And as the Lord hath his

---

From John Hale, *A Modest Inquiry into the Nature of Witchcraft*, reprinted in *Narratives of the Witchcraft Cases*, edited by G. L. Burr (New York, 1914), pp. 399–432.

Mysteries to bring us to Eternal Glory; so Satan hath his Mysteries to bring us to Eternal Ruine: Mysteries not easily understood, whereby the depths of Satan are managed in hidden wayes. So the Whore of Babylon makes the Inhabitants of the Earth drunk with the Wine of her Fornication, by the Mystery of her abominations, Rev. 17. 2. And the man of Sin hath his Mystery of iniquity whereby he deceiveth men through the working of Satan in signes and lying wonders, 2 Thes. 2. 3, 7, 9.

And among Satans Mysteries of iniquity, this of Witchcraft is one of the most difficult to be searched out by the Sons of men; as appeareth by the great endeavours of Learned and Holy men to search it out, and the great differences that are found among them, in the rules laid down for the bringing to light these hidden works of darkness. So that it may seem presumption in me to undertake so difficult a Theam, and to lay down such rules as are different from the Sentiments of many Eminent writers, and from the Precedents and practices of able Lawyers; yea and from the Common Law it self.

But my Apology for this undertaking is;

1. That there hath been such a dark dispensation by the Lord, letting loose upon us the Devil, *Anno.* 1692, as we never experienced before: And thereupon apprehending and condemning persons for Witchcraft; and nextly acquitting others no less liable to such a charge; which evidently shew we were in the dark, and knew not what to do; but have gone too far on the one or other side, if not on both. Hereupon I esteemed it necessary for some person to Collect a summary of that affair, with some animadversions upon it, which might at least give some light to them which come after, to shun those Rocks by which we were bruised, and narrowly escaped Shipwrack upon. And I have waited five years for some other person to undertake it, who might doe it better than I can, but find none; and judge it better to do what I can, than that such a work should be left undone. Better sincerely though weakly done, then not at all, or with such a byas of prejudice as will put false glosses upon that which was managed with uprightness of heart, though there was not so great a spirit of discerning, as were to be wished in so weighty a Concernment.

2. I have been present at several Examinations and Tryals, and knew sundry of those that Suffered upon that account in former years, and in this last affair, and so have more advantages than a stranger, to give account of these Proceedings.

3. I have been from my Youth trained up in the knowledge and belief of most of those principles I here question as unsafe to be used. The first person that suffered on this account in New-England, about Fifty years since, was my Neighbour, and I heard much of what was charged upon her, and others in those times; and the reverence I bore to aged, learned and judicious persons,

caused me to drink in their principles in these things, with a kind of Implicit Faith. *Quo semel est imbuta recens servabit odorem, Testa diu.* [Translation: "The fresh-made pot will long retain the odor in which once 'tis steeped."] A Child will not easily forsake the principles he hath been trained up in from his Cradle.

But observing the Events of that sad Catastrophe, *Anno* 1692, I was brought to a more strict scanning of the principles I had imbibed, and by scanning, to question, and by questioning at length to reject many of them, upon the reasons shewed in the ensuing Discourse. It is an approved saying *Nihil certius, quam quod ex dubio fit certum*; [Translation: "Nothing is surer than what out of doubt is made sure."] No truth more certain to a man, than that which he hath formerly doubted or denied, and is recovered from his error, by the convincing evidence of Scripture and reason. Yet I know and am sensible, that while we know but in part, man is apt in flying from a discovered error, to run into the contrary extream.

Incidit in Scyllam qui vult vitare Charybdim.
[Translation: "Into Scylla falls he who tries to keep clear of Charybdis."]

The middle way is commonly the way of truth. And if any can shew me a better middle way than I have here laid down, I shall be ready to embrace it: But the conviction must not be by vinegar or drollery, but by strength of argument.

4. I have had a deep sence of the sad consequence of mistakes in matters Capital; and their impossibility of recovering when compleated. And what grief of heart it brings to a tender conscience, to have been unwittingly encouraging of the Sufferings of the innocent. And I hope a zeal to prevent for the future such sufferings is pardonable, although there should be much weakness, and some errors in the pursuit thereof.

5. I observe the failings that have been on the one hand, have driven some into that which is indeed an extream on the other hand, and of dangerous consequences, *viz.* To deny any such persons to be under the New Testament, who by the Devils aid discover Secrets, or do work wonders. Therefore in the latter part of this discourse, I have taken pains to prove the Affirmative, yet with brevity, because it hath been done already by Perkins of *Witchcraft.* Glanvil his *Saducismus Triumphatus,* Pt. 1 p. 1 to 90 and Pt. 2 p. 1 to 80. Yet I would not be understood to justify all his notions in those discourses, but acknowledge he hath strongly proved the being of Witches.

6. I have special reasons moving me to bear my testimony about these matters, before I go hence and be no more; the which I have here done, and I

hope with some assistance of his Spirit, to whom I commit my self and this my labour, even that God whose I am and whom I serve: Desiring his Mercy in Jesus Christ to Pardon all the Errors of his People in the day of darkness; and to enable us to fight with Satan by Spiritual Weapons, putting on the whole Armour of God.

And tho' Satan by his Messengers may buffet Gods Children, yet there's a promise upon right *Resisting, he shall flee from them,* Jam. 4. 7. *And that all things shall work together for the good of those that Love the Lord,* Rom. 8. 28. So that I believe Gods Children shall be gainers by the assaults of Satan, which occasion'd this Discourse; which that they may, is the Prayer of, Thine in the Service of the Gospel.

* * *

I shall conclude this Discourse with some Application of the whole.

1. We may hence see ground to fear, that there hath been a great deal of innocent blood shed in the Christian World, by proceeding upon unsafe principles, in condemning persons for Malefick Witchcraft.

2. That there have been great sinful neglects in sparing others, who by their divinings about things future, or discovering things secret, as stollen Goods, etc., or by their informing of persons and things absent at a great distance, have implored the assistance of a familiar spirit, yet coloured over with specious pretences, and have drawn people to enquire of them: A sin frequently forbidden in Scripture, as Lev. 19. 31 and 20. 6, Isa. 8. 19, 20. and yet let alone, and in many parts of the World, have been countenanced in their diabolical skill and profession; because they serve the interest of those that have a vain curiosity, to pry into things God hath forbidden, and concealed from discovery by lawful means. And of others that by their inchantments, have raised mists, strange sights, and the like, to beget admiration, and please Spectators, etc., Whereas these divinations and operations are the Witchcraft more condemned in Scripture than the other.

3. But to come nigher home, we have cause to be humbled for the mistakes and errors which have been in these Colonies, in their Proceedings against persons for this crime, above fourty years ago and downwards, upon insufficient presumptions and precedents of our Nation, whence they came. I do not say, that all those were innocent, that suffered in those times upon this account. But that such grounds were then laid down to proceed upon, which were too slender to evidence the crime they were brought to prove; and

thereby a foundation laid to lead into error those that come after. May we not say in this matter, as it is, Psal. 106. 6. *We have sinned with our fathers?* And as, Lam. 5. 7. *Our fathers have sinned and are not, and we have born their iniquities?* And whether this be not one of the sins the Lord hath been many years contending with us for, is worthy our serious enquiry. If the Lord punished Israel with famine three years for a sin of misguided zeal fourty years before that, committed by the breach of a Covenant made four hundred years before that: 2 Sam. 21. 1, 2, Why may not the Lord visit upon us the misguided zeal of our Predecessors about Witchcraft above fourty years ago, even when that Generation is gathered to their Fathers.

4. But I would come yet nearer to our own times, and bewail the errors and mistakes that have been in the year 1692. In the apprehending too many we may believe were innocent, and executing of some, I fear, not to have been condemned; by following such traditions of our fathers, maxims of the Common Law, and Precedents and Principles, which now we may see weighed in the Balance of the Sanctuary, are found too light. I heartily concur with the Direction for our publick prayers, emitted December 17, 1696, by our General Assembly, in an order for a general Fast, *viz.* "That God would shew us what we know not, and help us wherein we have done amiss, to do so no more: And especially that whatever mistakes on either hand, have been fallen into, either by the body of this people, or any other of men, referring to the late tragedy raised among us by Satan and his Instruments, through the awful Judgment of God: He would humble us therefore, and pardon all the errors of his Servants and People, that desire to love his Name, and be attoned to his land." I am abundantly satisfyed that those who were most concerned to act and judge in those matters, did not willingly depart from the rules of righteousness. But such was the darkness of that day, the tortures and lamentations of the afflicted, and the power of former precedents, that we walked in the clouds, and could not see our way. And we have most cause to be humbled for error on that hand, which cannot be retrieved. So that we must beseech the Lord, that if any innocent blood hath been shed, in the hour of temptation, the Lord will not lay it to our charge, but be merciful to his people whom he hath redeemed. Deut. 21. 8, And that in the day when he shall visit, he will not visit this sin upon our land, but blot it out, and wash it away with the blood of Jesus Christ.

5. I would humbly propose whether it be not expedient, that some what more should be publickly done then yet hath, for clearing the good name and reputation of some that have suffered upon this account, against whom the evidence of their guilt was more slender, and the grounds for charity for them more convincing. And this (in order to our obtaining from the Lord farther

reconcilliation to our land,) and that none of their surviving relations, may suffer reproach upon that account. I have both read and heard of several in England, that have been executed for Capital crimes, and afterwards upon sense of an error in the process against them, have been restored in blood and honour by some publick act. My Lord Cook relates a story. A man going to correct a Girle his Neice, for some offence, in an upper room, the Girle strove to save her self, till her nose bled, and wiping it with a cloath, threw the bloody cloath out at the window, and cryed Murder; and then ran down staires, got away and hid her self. Her Uncle was prosecuted by her friends upon suspicion of Murdering her, because she could not be found. He declared that she made her escape, as above said. Then time was allowed him to bring her forth, but he could not hear of her within the time, and fearing he should dy if she could not be found, procures another Girle very like her, to appear in Court, and declare she was his Neice that had been missing: But her relations examine this counterfeit, until they find her out, and she confesseth she was suborned and counterfeited the true Niece. Upon these presumptions the man was found guilty of Murdering his Neice, and thereupon executed. And after his execution his true Neice comes abroad and shews her self alive and well. Then all that saw it were convinced of the Uncles innocency, and vanity of such presumptions. The Printing and Publishing of this relation Vindicates the good name of the Uncle, from the imputation of the crime of Murder. And this is one end of this present discourse, to take off (so far as a discourse of this nature can) infamy from the names and memory of such sufferers in this kind, as do not deserve the same.

6. Here it may be suitable for us to enquire, What the Lord speaks to us by such a stupendeous providence, in his letting loose Satan upon us in this unusual way? *Ans.* 1. We may say of this, as our Saviour said of his washing his disciples feet, Joh. 13. *What I do thou knowest not now, but thou shalt know hererafter. The Judgments of the Lord are a great deep,* Psal. 36. 6. *How unsearchable are his judgments, and his ways past finding out.* 2. Yet somewhat of his counsel at present for our instruction may be known, by comparing the Word and works of God together.

1. As when Joshua the high Priest though an holy chosen man of God, stood before the Angel, Satan stood at his right hand to resist him, or to be his adversary: And the advantage Satan had was by the filthy garments Joshua was clothed with before the Angels: That is, some iniquity which yet was not passed away, Zech. 3. 1, 3, 4. So we may say here were among Gods own Children filthy garments. The sins of Lukewarmness, loss of our first love, unprofitableness under the Gospel, slumbering and sleeping in the wise, as well as foolish Virgins, worldliness, pride, carnal security, and many other

sins. By these and such like sins the accuser of the Brethren [i.e., Satan] got advantage to stand at our right hand (the place of an Accuser in Courts of Justice) and there accuse us and resist us.

2. When the Egyptians refused to let Israel go to sacrifice and keep a feast to the Lord in the Wilderness: The Lord cast upon [them] the fierceness of his wrath, by sending Evil Angels among them, Psal. 78. 49. Egypts sins were (1.) Coveteousness; they would not let Israel go, because they gained by their labours. (2.) Contempt of God and his Instituted Worship, and Ordinances. They did not count them of such concernment, that Israel should go into the Wilderness to observe them. Both these sins have too much increased in our Land. (1.) Coveteousness, an inordinate love of the World gave Satan advantage upon us. (2.) Contempt of Gods Worship and Instituted Ordinances. The Errand of our Fathers into this Wilderness, was to Sacrifice to the Lord; that is, to worship God in purity of heart and life, and to wait upon the Lord, walking in the faith and order of the Gospel in Church fellowship; that they might enjoy Christ in all his Ordinances. But these things have been greatly neglected and despised by many born, or bred up in the Land. We have much forgotten what our Fathers came into the Wilderness to see. The sealing Ordinances of the Covenant of Grace in Church-Communion have been much slighted and neglected; and the fury of this Storm raised by Satan hath fallen very heavily upon many that lived under these neglects. The Lord sends Evil Angels to awaken and punish our negligence: And to my knowledge some have been hereby excited to enter into the Chamber of Gods Ordinances, to hide themselves, until the indignation be over past.

3. David when he removed the Ark from Kirjathjearim, had the Ark put into a new Cart, which should have been carried by the Kohathites. Numb. 3.31. And David thought this was right, until the Lord slew Uzza for touching the Ark: But then he looked more exactly into the will of God; and confesseth that the Lord made a breach upon them, because they sought him not after the due order, 1 Chron. 13. 5, 7, 9, 10, and 15. 11, 12, 13. Had not the Lord made that breach upon them, they had persisted securely in their error. So I may say in this case. In the prosecution of Witchcraft, we sought not the Lord after the due order; but have proceeded after the methods used in former times and other places, until the Lord in this tremendous way made a breach upon us. And hereby we are made sensible that the methods formerly used are not sufficient to prove the guilt of such a crime. And this I conceive was one end of the Lords letting Satan loose to torment and accuse so many; that hereby we may search out the truth more exactly. For had it not been for this dreadful dispensation, many would have lived and dyed in that error, which they are now convinced of.

4. The Lord delivered into the hand of Satan the Estate, Children, and Body of Job, for the tryal of Jobs faith and patience, and proof of his perfection and uprightness. So the Lord hath delivered into Satans hand mens Children and Bodies, yea names and estates into Satans hand for the tryal of their faith and patience, and farther manifestation of the sincerity of their professions.

7. From that part of the discourse which shews the power of Satan to torment the bodies, and disturb the minds of those, he is let loose upon. . . . I would infer, that Satan may be suffered so to darken the minds of some pious Souls, as to cause them to destroy themselves by drowning, hanging, or the like. And when he hath so far prevailed upon some, that formerly lived a Christian life, but were under the prevalency of a distracting Melancholy at their latter end, We may have Charity that their Souls are Saved, notwithstanding the sad conclusion of their lives. I speak not to excuse any that having the free use of their reason willingly destroy themselves, out of pride, discontent, impatience, etc. Achitophel who out of height of Spirit because his Counsel was not followed, and to prevent Davids executing of him, for his rebellion and treason, destroyed himself, hath left his name to stink unto all generations. And Judas who for his unparalelled treachery in betraying his Master, and the Lord of life, was justly left to hange himself; and the rope breaking or slipping he fell down head long, or with his face down ward, so that he burst asunder in the midst, and all his bowels gushed out, Math. 27. 5. with Act. 1. 13, left by his sin and punishment in the last act of his life the black character of a Son of perdition. But those that being out of their right minds, and hurried by an evil Spirit, as persons under a force to be their own executioners, are not always to be ranked with these.

8. Seeing we have been too fierce against supposed Malefick Witchcraft, let us take heed we do not on the contrary become too favourable to divining Witchcraft: And become like Saul who was too zealous against the Gibeonites, and at last turned to seek after one that had a familiar Spirit, to his own destruction. Let us not, if we can help it, suffer Satan to set up an ensuring office for stolen Goods. That after he hath brought the curse of God into the house of the thief, by tempting him to steal, he may not bring about the curse into the houses of them from whom the goods were stolen, by alluring them to go to the god of Ekron to enquire. That men may not give their Souls to the Devil in exchange, for his restoring to them their goods again, in such a way of divination. The Lord grant it may be said of New England, as is prophecyed of Judah, Mich. 5. 12. *I will cut off Witchcrafts out of thine hand, and thou shalt have no more soothsayers.*

9. Another extream we must beware of, is, *viz*. Because our fathers in the beginning times of this Land, did not see so far into these mysteries of iniquity, as hath been since discovered, Let us not undervalue the good foundations they laid for God and his people, and for us in Church and Civil Government. For Paul that eminent Apostle knew but in part; no wonder then, if our Fathers were imperfect men. In the purest times in Israel, there were some Clouds of ignorance over-shadowing of them. Abraham, David, and the best Patriarchs were generally ignorant of the sin of Polygamy. And although Solomon far exceeded Nehemiah in wisdom; yet Nehemiah saw farther into the evil of Marrying Outlandish Women, than that wisest of Kings, and meer fallen men. Neh. 13. 26. Josiah kept the Passeover more exactly, than David, and all the Reforming Kings of Judah, 2 Chron. 35. 18.

All the godly Judges and Kings of Judah were unacquainted with, and so negligent of the right observation of the feast of Tabernacles, until it came to Nehemiahs time: And he understood and revived an ordinance of God, that lay buried in oblivion, near about a thousand years. Now he that shall reject all the good in doctrine and practice, which was maintained, professed and practiced by so many Godly leaders, because of some few errors found among them, will be found to fight against God. A dwarf upon a giants shoulders, can see farther than the giant.

It was a glorious enterprize of the beginners of these Colonies, to leave their native Country to propagate the Gospel: And a very high pitch of faith, zeal, and courage that carried them forth, to follow the Lord into this wilderness, into a land that was not sown. Then was New England holiness to the Lord, and all that did devour them, or attempted so to do, did offend, and evil did come upon them. And the Lord did graciously remember this kindness of their Youth, and love of their Espousals; In granting them many eminent tokens of his favour; by his presence with them in his Ordinances, for the Conversion of Souls, and edifying and comforting the hearts of his Servants: By signal answering their prayers in times of difficulty: By protecting them from their Enemies; By guiding of, and providing for them in a Desart. And the Lord will still remember this their kindness unto their Posterity, unless that by their Apostasy from the Lord, they vex his Holy Spirit, to turn to be their Enemy: And thereby cast off the Entail of his Covenant Mercies; which God forbid. *Oh that the Lord may be with us, as he was with our Fathers; and that he may not leave us, nor forsake us!*

Fixing the Blame

CHARLES W. UPHAM (1802–1875) was a prominent citizen of Salem who served the community as minister, mayor, and U.S. congressman. Upham also had a lifelong interest in the history of his town, and in 1867 he published the results of his research in two volumes entitled Salem Witchcraft.

In the selection that follows, Upham accuses the "afflicted girls" of deliberately and callously bringing about the death of their neighbors; and he suggests that the girls were guided in this wickedness by adults seeking revenge or personal gain.

To the modern reader, Upham's massive study seems poorly organized and rambling. And his thesis that the girls were lying was hardly new—Robert Calef hinted at the same conclusion in 1697. Upham's conspiracy thesis was soon challenged on the grounds that a sustained plot by young girls was too improbable to believe. Other writers criticized his one-dimensional view of the Puritan clergy, and cited in particular his bitter attack on Cotton Mather. Nevertheless, it was Upham's version of the witchcraft outbreak that became the standard interpretation, repeated for generations in textbooks on American history. And even those historians who disagreed with aspects of Upham's argument, by and large shared his belief that some individual or group could be blamed for the Salem tragedy.

6. The Afflicted Girls Were Lying

What are we to think of those persons who commenced and continued the accusations—the "afflicted children" and their associates?

In some instances and to some extent, the steps they took and the testimony they bore may be explained by referring to the mysterious energies of the imagination, the power of enthusiasm, the influence of sympathy, and the general prevalence of credulity, ignorance, superstition, and fanaticism at the time; and it is not probable, that, when they began, they had any idea of the tremendous length to which they were finally led on.

It was perhaps their original design to gratify a love of notoriety or of mischief by creating a sensation and excitement in their neighborhood, or, at the worst, to wreak their vengence upon one or two individuals who had offended them. They soon, however, became intoxicated by the terrible

From Charles W. Upham, *Salem Witchcraft* (2 vols., Boston, 1867).

success of their imposture, and were swept along by the frenzy they had occasioned. It would be much more congenial with our feelings to believe, that these misguided and wretched young persons early in the proceedings became themselves victims of the delusion into which they plunged every one else. But we are forbidden to form this charitable judgment by the manifestations of art and contrivance, of deliberate cunning and cool malice, they exhibited to the end. Once or twice they were caught in their own snare; and nothing but the blindness of the bewildered community saved them from disgraceful exposure and well-deserved punishment. They appeared as the prosecutors of every poor creature that was tried, and seemed ready to bear testimony against any one upon whom suspicion might happen to fall. It is dreadful to reflect upon the enormity of their wickedness, if they were conscious of imposture throughout. It seems to transcend the capabilities of human crime. There is, perhaps, a slumbering element in the heart of man, that sleeps for ever in the bosom of the innocent and good, and requires the perpetration of a great sin to wake it into action, but which, when once aroused, impels the transgressor onward with increasing momentum, as the descending ball is accelerated in its course. It may be that crime begets an appetite for crime, which, like all other appetites, is not quieted but inflamed by gratification.

Their precise moral condition, the degree of guilt to be ascribed, and the sentence to be passed upon them, can only be determined by a considerate review of all the circumstances and influences around them.

For a period embracing about two months, they had been in the habit of meeting together, and spending the long winter evenings, at Mr. Parris's house, practising the arts of fortune-telling, jugglery, and magic. What they had heard in the traditions and fables of a credulous and superstitious age— stories handed down in the interior settlements, circulated in companies gathered around the hearths of farmhouses, indulging the excitements of terrified imaginations; filling each others's minds with wondrous tales of second-sight, ghosts and spirits from the unseen world, together with what the West-Indian or South-American slaves could add—was for a long time the food of their fancies. They experimented continually upon what was the spiritualism of their day, and grew familiar with the imagery and the exhibitions of the marvellous. The prevalent notions concerning witchcraft operations and spectral manifestations came into full effect among them. Living in the constant contemplation of such things, their minds became inflamed and bewildered; and, at the same time, they grew expert in practising and exhibiting the forms of pretended supernaturalism, the conditions of diabolical distraction, and the terrors of demonology. Apparitions rose before them, revealing the secrets of the past and of the future. They beheld the present spectres of persons then bodily far distant. They declared in language, fits, dreams, or trance, the immediate operations upon themselves of the Devil, by the agency of his confederates. Their sufferings, while thus under "an evil hand," were dreadful to behold, and soon drew wondering and horror-struck crowds around them.

At this point, if Mr. Parris, the ministers, and magistrates had done their duty, the mischief might have been stopped. The girls ought to have been rebuked for their dangerous and forbidden sorceries and divinations, their meetings broken up, and all such tamperings with alleged supernaturalism and spiritualism frowned down. Instead of this, the neighboring ministers were summoned to meet at Mr. Parris's house to witness the extraordinary doings of the girls, and all they did was to indorse, and pray over, them. Countenance was thus given to their pretensions, and the public confidence in the reality of their statements established. Magistrates from the town, church-members, leading people, and people of all sorts, flocked to witness the awful power of Satan, as displayed in the tortures and contortions of the "afflicted children;" who became objects of wonder, so far as their feats were regarded, and of pity in view of their agonies and convulsions.

The aspect of the evidence rather favors the supposition, that the girls originally had no design of accusing, or bringing injury upon, any one. But the ministers at Parris's house, physicians and others, began the work of destruction by pronouncing the opinion that they were bewitched. This carried with it, according to the received doctrine, a conviction that there were witches about; for the Devil could not act except through the instrumentality of beings in confederacy with him. Immediately, the girls were beset by everybody to say who it was that bewitched them. Yielding to this pressure, they first cried out upon such persons as might have been most naturally suggested to them—Sarah Good, apparently without a regular home, and wandering with her children from house to house for shelter and relief; Sarah Osburn, a melancholy, broken-minded, bed-ridden person; and Tituba, a slave, probably of mixed African and Indian blood. At the examination of these persons, the girls were first brought before the public, and the awful power in their hands revealed to them. The success with which they acted their parts; the novelty of the scene; the ceremonials of the occasion, the magistrates in their imposing dignity and authority, the trappings of the marshal and his officers, the forms of proceeding,—all which they had never seen before; the notice taken of them; the importance attached to them; invested the affair with a strange fascination in their eyes, and awakened a new class of sentiments and ideas in their minds. A love of distinction and notoriety, and the several passions that are gratified by the expression by others of sympathy, wonder, and admiration, were brought into play. The fact that all eyes were upon them, with the special notice of the magistrates, and the entire confidence with which their statements were received, flattered and beguiled them. A fearful responsibility had been assumed, and they were irretrievably committed to their position. While they adhered to that position, their power was irresistible, and they were sure of the public sympathy and of being cherished by the public favor. If they faltered, they would be the objects of universal execration and of the severest penalties of law for the wrongs already done and the falsehoods already sworn to. There was no retracing their steps; and their only safety was in continuing the excitement they had raised. New victims were constantly required to prolong the delusion, fresh fuel to keep up the conflagration; and they went on to cry out upon others. With the exception of two of their number, who appear to have indulged spite against the families in which they were servants, there is no evidence that they were actuated by private grievances or by animosities personal to themselves. They were ready and sure to wreak vengeance upon any who expressed doubts about the truth of their testimony, or the propriety of the proceedings; but, beyond this, they were very indifferent as to whom they should accuse. They were willing, as to that matter, to follow the suggestions of others, and availed themselves of all the gossip and slander and unfriendly talk in their families that reached their ears. It was found, that a hint, with a little information as to persons, places, and circumstances, conveyed to them by those who had resentments and grudges to gratify, would be sufficient for the purpose. There is reason to fear, that there were some behind them, giving direction to the accusations, and managing the frightful machinery, all the way through. The persons who were apprehended had, to a considerable extent, been obnoxious, and subject to prejudice, in connection with quarrels and controversies related in Part I., vol. i.* They were "Topsfield men," or the opponents of Bayley or of Parris, or more or less connected with some other feuds. As further proof that the girls were under the guidance of older heads, it is obvious, that there was, in the order of the proceedings, a skilful arrangement of times, sequences, and concurrents, that cannot be ascribed to them. No novelist or dramatist ever laid his plot deeper, distributed his characters more artistically, or conducted more methodically the progress of his story.

In the mean while, they were becoming every day more perfect in the

---

Editor's note: Part I, vol. i of Upham's *Salem Witchcraft* deals with antagonisms in the village that predated the trials. Among these were the boundary dispute with the neighboring town of Topsfield and a disagreement involving two ministers, James Bayley and Samuel Parris. These episodes had created lasting scars.

performance of their parts; and their imaginative powers, nervous excitability, and flexibility and rapidity of muscular action, were kept under constant stimulus, and attaining a higher development. The effect of these things, so long continued in connection with the perpetual pretence, becoming more or less imbued with the character of belief, of their alliance and communion with spiritual beings and manifestations, may have unsettled, to some extent, their minds. Added to this, a sense of the horrid consequences of their actions, accumulating with every pang they inflicted, the innocent blood they were shedding, and the depths of ruin into which they were sinking themselves and others, not only demoralized, but to some extent, perhaps, crazed them. It is truly a marvel that their physical constitutions did not break down under the exhausting excitements, the contortions of frame, the force to which the bodily functions were subjected in trances and fits, and the strain upon all the vital energies, protracted through many months. The wonder, however, would have been greater, if the mental and moral balance had not thereby been disturbed.

Perpetual conversance with ideas of supernaturalism; daily and nightly communications, whether in the form of conscious imposture or honest delusion, with the spiritual world, continued through a great length of time—as much at least as the exclusive contemplation of any one idea or class of ideas—must be allowed to be unsalutary. Whatever keeps the thoughts wholly apart from the objects of real and natural life, and absorbs them in abstractions, cannot be favorable to the soundness of the faculties or the tone of the mind. This must especially be the effect, if the subjects thus monopolizing the attention partake of the marvellous and mysterious. When these things are considered, and the external circumstances of the occasion, the wild social excitement, the consternation, confusion, and horror, that were all crowded and heaped up and kept pressing upon the soul without intermission for months, the wonder is, indeed, that not only the accusers, prosecutors, and sufferers, but the whole people, did not lose their senses. Never was the great boon of life, a sound mind in a sound body, more liable to be snatched away from all parties. The depositions of Ann Putnam, Sr., have a tinge of sadness—a melancholy, sickly mania running through them. Something of the kind is, perhaps, more or less discernible in the depositions of others.

Let us, then, relieve our common nature from the load of the imputation, that, in its normal state, it is capable of such inconceivable wickedness, by giving to these wretched persons the benefit of the supposition that they were more or less deranged. This view renders the lesson they present more impressive and alarming. Sin in all cases, when considered by a mind that surveys the whole field, is itself insanity. In the case of these accusers, it was so great as to prove, by its very monstrousness, that it had actually subverted their nature and overthrown their reason. They followed their victims to the gallows, and jeered, scoffed, insulted them in their dying hours. Sarah Churchill, according to the testimony of Sarah Ingersoll, on one occasion came to herself, and manifested the symptoms of a restored moral conscious- ness: but it was a temporary gleam, a lucid interval; and she passed back into darkness, continuing, as before, to revel in falsehood, and scatter destruction around her. With this single exception, there is not the slightest appearance of compunction or reflection among them. On the contrary, they seem to have been in a frivolous, sportive, gay frame of thought and spirits. There is, perhaps, in this view of their conduct and demeanor, something to justify the belief that they were really demented. The fact that a large amount of skilful art and adroit cunning was displayed by them is not inconsistent with the supposition that they had become partially insane; for such cunning and art are often associated with insanity.

The quick wit and ready expedients of the "afflicted children" are very remarkable. They were prompt with answers, if any attempted to cross- examine them, extricated themselves most ingeniously if ever brought into embarrassment, and eluded all efforts to entrap or expose them. Among the papers is a deposition, the use of which at the trials is not apparent. It does not purport to bear upon any particular case. Joseph Hutchinson was a firm- minded man, of strong common sense. He would not easily be deceived; and, although he took part in the proceedings at the beginning, soon became opposed to them. It looks as if, by close questions put to the child, Abigail Williams, on some occasion of his casually meeting her, he had tried to expose the falseness of her accusations, and that he was made to put the conversation into the shape of a deposition. It is as follows:

"THE DEPOSITION OF JOSEPH HUTCHINSON, aged fifty-nine years, do tes- tify as followeth: Abigail Williams, I have heard you speak often of a book that has been offered to you. She said that there were two books: one was a short, thick book; and the other ̷as a long book. I asked her what color the book was of. She said the books were as red as blood. I asked her if she had seen the books opened. She said she had seen it many times. I asked her if she did see any writing in the book. She said there were many lines written; and, at the end of every line, there was a seal. I asked her, who brought the book to her. She told me that it was the black man. I asked her who the black man was. She told me it was the Devil. I asked her if she was not afraid to see the Devil. She said, at the first she was, and did go from him; but now she was not afraid, but could talk with him as well as she could with me."

There is an air of ease and confidence in the answers of Abigail, which illustrates the promptness of invention and assurance of their grounds which the girls manifested on all occasions. They were never at a loss, and challenged scrutiny. Hutchinson gained no advantage, and no one else ever did, in an encounter with them.

Whatever opinion may be formed of the moral or mental condition of the "afflicted children," as to their sanity and responsibility, there can be no doubt that they were great actors. In mere jugglery and sleight of hand, they bear no mean comparison with the workers of wonders, in that line, of our own day. Long practice had given them complete control over their countenances, intonations of voice,and the entire muscular and nervous organization of their bodies; so that they could at will, and on the instant, go into fits and convulsions, swoon and fall to the floor, put their frames into strange contortions, bring the blood to the face, and send it back again. They could be deadly pale at one moment, at the next flushed; their hands would be clenched and held together as with a vice; their limbs stiff and rigid or wholly relaxed; their teeth would be set; they would go through the paroxysms of choking and strangulation, and gasp for breath, bringing froth and blood from the mouth; they would utter all sorts of screams in unearthly tones; their eyes remain fixed, sometimes bereft of all light and expression, cold and stony, and sometimes kindled into flames of passion; they would pass into the state of somnambulism, without aim or conscious direction in their movements, looking at some point, where was no apparent object of vision, with a wild, unmeaning glare. There are some indications that they had acquired the art of ventriloquism; or they so wrought upon the imaginations of the beholders, that the sounds of the motions and voices of invisible beings were believed to be heard. They would start, tremble, and be pallid before apparitions, seen, of course, only by themselves; but their acting was so perfect that all present thought they saw them too. They would address and hold colloquy with spectres and ghosts; and the responses of the unseen beings would be audible to the fancy of the bewildered crowd. They would follow with their eyes the airy visions, so that others imagined they also beheld them. This was surely a high dramatic achievement. Their representations of pain, and every form and all the signs of marks of bodily suffering—as in the case of Ann Putnam's arm, and the indentations of teeth on the flesh in many instances—utterly deceived everybody; and there were men present who could not easily have been imposed upon. The Attorney-general was a barrister fresh from Inns of Court in London. Deodat Lawson had seen something of the world; so had Joseph Herrick. Joseph Hutchinson was a sharp, stern, and sceptical observer. John Putnam was a man of great practical force and discrimination; so was his brother Nathaniel, and others of the village. Besides, there were many from Boston and elsewhere competent to detect a trick; but none could discover any imposture in the girls. Sarah Nurse swore that she saw Goody Bibber cheat in the matter of the pins; but Bibber did not belong to the village, and was a bungling interloper. The accusing girls showed extraordinary skill, ingenuity, and fancy in inventing the stories to which they testified, and seemed to have been familiar with the imagery which belonged to the literature of demonology. This has led some to suppose that they must have had access to books treating the subject. Our fathers abhorred, with a perfect hatred, all theatrical exhibitions. It would have filled them with horror to propose going to a play. But unwittingly, week after week, month in and month out, ministers, deacons, brethren, and sisters of the church rushed to Nathaniel Ingersoll's, to the village and town meeting-houses, and to Thomas Beadle's Globe Tavern, and gazed with wonder, awe, and admiration upon acting such as has seldom been surpassed on the boards of any theatre, high or low, ancient or modern.

Because we no longer believe in the supernatural power of witches, we have assumed that the individuals executed in Salem were innocent. But CHADWICK HANSEN (b. 1926), a professor of American literature and American studies at the University of Illinois, raises another possibility. In the following essay (and more fully in his book Witchcraft at Salem) *he suggests that at least some of those who were executed might have thought themselves in league with the Devil and might have consciously tried to work black magic. And in a society that believes in witchcraft, the power of suggestion can make charms and spells quite effective—even fatal. This puts Salem in a new light. If some of the witches were guilty of the intent to do harm, then the trials were not entirely a mistake and the actions of the village residents were not entirey unjustifed.*

Cotton Mather, writing at the time of the outbreak, placed the blame squarely on the witches. One hundred and seventy-five years later, Upham placed the blame on the afflicted girls. Now, three centuries after Salem, Hansen has returned the focus to the witches. In this long process, has our understanding of what happened at Salem deepened, or are we simply moving in circles as we search for the guilty party?

7. Some of the Witches were Guilty

Witchcraft is not easy to define, because it is not, like the major formal religions, a coherent body of belief. But in Western civilization since prehis-

From Chadwick Hansen, "Salem Witches and DeForest's *Witching Times*," *Essex Institute Historical Collections*, vol. 104 (April 1968), no. 2, pp. 89–108. Copyright © 1968, by Essex Institute, Salem, Mass. 01970. Reprinted by permission of the Essex Institute. Footnotes omitted.

toric times there has been a loosely grouped body of magical lore—charms, spells and so forth—having to do primarily with fertility and infertility, and with health and sickness, as well as a series of more marginal concerns. Such lore has obvious, if tenuous, connections to pre-Christian fertility worship; thus it is not surprising that the tutelary deity of that lore should be a fertility god. I suppose the commonest of fertility gods has been the deified sun, but the next most common has been the deified herd animal—the cow, or, more often (because of his reputation for lechery), the goat. Half human and half bestial, with horns and cloven hooves, he appeared as Dionysus or Bacchus, the chief fertility god of the classical world, and had appeared as well in the pantheons of Northern Europe. Apparently the early Christians thought him the most abominable of all the pagan deities, because they gave his attributes, his horns and cloven hooves, to the Devil, adding to them the wings of the fallen angel.

I am not suggesting that everyone who has used a charm was a formal worshipper of the Devil. Not much more than two centuries ago, however, everyone who used a charm believed he was making an appeal to dangerous occult forces, and making it at possible peril to his soul. But the degree of peril was relative, and proportionate to the degree of witchcraft, which, like murder, comes in three degrees.

The first involves the practice of white magic—charms or spells used for benevolent purposes. Carrying a rabbit's foot (the rabbit, like the goat, is notorious for its fertility) is white magic. So is nailing a horseshoe over the door (the open end must be upward, so the shape will suggest the horns of the herd animal). Since the intention was innocent, the practice of white magic was seldom a cause for official concern. It was, of course, an appeal to occult forces that were specifically non-Christian. Thus it could, and sometimes did, draw a stern verbal rebuke from the clergy. But that was all.

The second degree of witchcraft is black magic—magic used maliciously— and in the seventeenth century black magic was very serious indeed; it was an appeal to the Prince of Evil in order to accomplish evil. And the third degree of witchcraft is pact, where the witch is no longer merely invoking the Devil's aid through her charms and spells, but actually believes that she has made a contract to serve him. I know that the popular view, and the view even of most historians, is that no witchcraft was practiced in New England. But this view is mistaken. It can be demonstrated that all three degrees of witchcraft were practiced there during the latter seventeenth century: white magic commonly, black magic not uncommonly, and pact on at least one occasion. . . .

And we must remember that in a society which believes in witchcraft, witchcraft works. If you believe in witchcraft and you discover that someone has been melting your wax image over a slow fire or muttering charms over your nail-pairings, the probability is that you will get extremely sick. To be sure, your symptoms will be psychosomatic rather than organic. But the fact that they are obviously not organic will make them only more terrible, since they will seem the result of malefic and demonic power. And so it was in seventeenth-century Massachusetts.

The hideous convulsive fits were thought to be the result of witches and demons wrenching the bodies of their victims into tortuous postures. The losses of hearing, speech, sight, appetite and memory were deprivations caused by Satan himself. The contraction of the throat—the *globus hystericus*—was seen as an attempt by demons to make the victim swallow occult poisons. And when the victim swallowed rapidly and his belly swelled (what is actually involved here is a kind of accelerated ulcer formation), it was thought the demons had succeeded. When blisters appeared upon the skin (many skin diseases are functional rather than organic), they were thought to have been raised by brimstone out of Hell. To be sure, many of these symptoms, including the skin lesions, would pass fairly rapidly. Cotton Mather, who was a Fellow of the Royal Society, a former medical student, and a thorough and careful observer, remarked more than once on the surprising rapidity with which "witch-wounds" healed. But other symptoms would persist. And a new fit would bring a repetition of the old symptoms, or new ones equally alarming.

The cause of these hysterical symptoms, of course, was not witchcraft itself but the victim's fear of it, and that is why so many innocent persons were executed. It is impossible now, and was in many instances impossible then, to tell how many of the persons executed for witchcraft were actually guilty of practicing it. It is surely no exaggeration to say that the majority, even the vast majority, were innocent victims of hysterical fears. But we should again be wary of converting a statistical truth into a general principle. While it is clearly true that the majority of persons executed for witchcraft were innocent, it is equally true that some of them, in Massachusetts and elsewhere, were guilty.

* * *

Contrary to popular opinion, New England's record in regard to witchcraft is surprisingly good, as Thomas Hutchinson pointed out: "more having been put to death in a single county in England, in a short space of time, than have suffered in all New England from the first settlement until the present time [1750]." And through most of the seventeenth century the record is really astonishing. While Europe hanged and burned literally thousands of witches, executions in New England were few and far between. In part this record may be due to the New Englander's conviction that he belonged to a chosen people. God, many thought, would not permit Satan to afflict the elect. There would be no demonic terrors in Zion. But this belief was shattered in the year 1688, when a practicing witch was caught in Boston.

Her name was Goodwife Glover. She was brought to trial on the complaint of John Goodwin, the father of the children she "afflicted," and a concise account of that trial is given in Cotton Mather's *Memorable Providences:*

> It was long before she could with any Direct Answers plead unto her Indictment; and when she did plead, it was with Confession rather than Denial or her Guilt. Order was given to search the old womans house, from whence there were brought into the Court, several small Images, or Puppets, or Babies, made of Raggs, and stuff't with Goat's hair, and other such Ingredients. When these were produced, the vile Woman acknowledged, that her way to torment the Objects of her malice, was by wetting of her Finger with her Spittle, and stroaking of those little Images. The abused Children were then present, and the Woman still kept stooping and shrinking as one that was almost prest to Death with a mighty Weight upon her. But one of the Images being brought unto her, immediately she started up after an odd manner, and took it into her hand; but she had no sooner taken it, than one of the Children fell into sad Fits, before the whole Assembly. This the Judges had their just Apprehensions at; and carefully causing the Repetition of the Experiment, found again the same event of it. They asked her, Whether she had any to stand by her [i.e., character witnesses]: She replied, She had: and looking very pertly in the Air, she added, No, he's gone. And then she confessed, that she had One, who was her Prince, with whom she maintain'd, I know not what Communion. For which cause, the night after, she was heard expostulating with a Devil, for his thus deserting her; telling him that Because he had served her so basely and falsely, she had confessed all. However to make all clear, The Court appointed five or six Physicians one evening to examine her very strictly, whether she were not craz'd in her Intellectuals, and had not procured to her self by Folly and Madness the Reputation of a Witch. Diverse hours did they spend with her; and in all that while no Discourse came from her, but what was pertinent and agreeable: particularly, when they asked her, What she thought would become of her soul? she reply'd "You ask me a very solemn Question, and I cannot well tell what to say to it." She own'd her self a Roman Catholick; and could recite her Pater Noster very readily; but there was one Clause or two alwaies too hard for her, whereof she said, "She could not repeat it, if

she might have all the world.'' In the upshot, the Doctors returned her Compos Mentis; and sentence of Death was pass'd upon her.

I doubt that there has ever been a more clear-cut case of witchcraft.Image magic is the commonest form of black magic. The impulse behind it survives even when the belief in magic is gone, as anyone knows who has ever torn up the photograph of a person with whom they are angry. (College students are obeying the same impulse when they hang or burn someone in effigy, and it is worth noticing that hanging and burning were the means of executing witches. Nobody is ever shot, or gassed or electrocuted in effigy.) The dolls were stuffed with goat's hair because it is the goat who is deified in Satan's horns and cloven hooves. Spittle was applied to them because spittle was believed to have occult power (a belief that still survives in our expression about spitting on the hands before undertaking a particularly arduous task). To determine whether or not the plea should be insanity, the defendant was examined by a committee of physicians, who agreed that she was sane.

Plainly she believed that she had made a pact with Satan. When she was asked who would stand by her, she attempted to call on him, and she was overheard at night, in her cell, berating him for having abandoned her.But what is most important is that her witchcraft plainly worked, and in no indiscriminate fashion. When she tormented one of her dolls, *one* of the Goodwin children "fell into sad fits." When it is remembered that the violent hysterical symptoms to which the Goodwin children were subject not infrequently terminate in death, I do not think it can be said that the Boston court acted either harshly or unjustly. Indeed, when one considers the ferocity of seventeenth-century English law, simple hanging becomes almost a lenient sentence for what Goodwife Glover had done.

It is worth noticing Cotton Mather's handling of his part in the Glover case. Before she died the confessed witch gave to him the names of four persons whom she said had joined with her in worshipping Satan. They were, he tells us in his writings, disreputable persons. But he refused to make their names public, on the excellent grounds that one should not accept the testimony of a confessed witch. The history of witchcraft in Salem (and, indeed, of many other "witch-hunts") would have been very different if this principle had been generally followed. Mather also undertook the cure of the afflicted children, taking the eldest of them into his own house. In the midst of their fits the children accused several people of afflicting them, but again Mather refused to make the names of the accused public, on the ground that children in fits are not reliable witnesses. They may be deluded, he thought, or the Devil may be speaking through them. This principle also might profitably have been followed at Salem. (The picturesque belief that the Devil might be speaking through the afflicted children was founded on the fact that these children sometimes did speak in voices, human or bestial, that were clearly not their own. The phenomenon was plainly an instance of multiple personality, the extreme form of the hysterical fugue.)

For our immediate purposes, however, the most important consequence of the Glover case was that it demonstrated clearly that witchcraft did exist in Massachusetts, and witchcraft of the most serious and dangerous sort. The Devil was abroad in Zion, seeking whom he might devour.

* * *

When he broke forth again, at Salem Village in 1692, we have seen the first consequences: the children's alarming fits and Doctor Griggs' eventual diagnosis of witchcraft. Following such a diagnosis it was most natural to ask the children who was afflicting them. But at first, apparently, they were not able to answer, and their relatives feared that the Devil was preventing them from speaking. At least this was the conclusion of Mary Sibly, the aunt of one of the afflicted girls, who had recourse to white magic in order to break the Devil's spell. She went to Tituba and her husband John, two West Indian slaves of the Reverend Mr. Parris, and had them prepare a witch-cake out of rye meal and the urine of the children (urine, like spittle, was supposed to have occult power). The cake was baked, and fed to the Parris dog, presumably on the theory that he was a familiar—an agent who communicated between the Devil and a witch.

The minister was appalled, when he discovered what had happened. He lectured Mrs. Sibley both privately and before the entire congregation on the sinfulness of using the Devil's methods to find out the Devil, and she acknowledged her sinfulness in tears. But it was too late; the damage had been done. The witch-cake worked—another instance of the efficacy of magic in a society which believes in it. The girls were able to name their afflicters: Tituba herself, and Sarah Good and Sarah Osborne-two women of dubious reputation. And when Tituba was examined on March 1 by John Hathorne (his descendant, Nathaniel, added the "w") and Jonathan Corwin, two magistrates of Salem Town, she almost immediately confessed, implicating Goodwives Good and Osborne as well as three persons whom she could not identify—two women and "a tall man of Boston." That was the beginning of it. By the end of the month accusations were becoming general. The ranks of the afflicted had increased; so had those of the confessors.

Nothing is at first sight more surprising than the number of confessors. By the time the witchcraft was over there were more than fifty of them. Robert Calef maintains that Parris beat Tituba into confessing. Perhaps he did; furthermore, there is strong evidence to suggest that several others were bullied into confessing. Others, as we know from the evidence of some who recanted, confessed to save their lives; it had become obvious early in the trials that confessors would not be executed. But the majority of the confessors were apparently hysterics, like the afflicted girls. Certainly that is the implication to be drawn from Thomas Brattle's "Letter." "As to about thirty of these fifty-five Confessours, they are possessed (I reckon) with the Devill, and afflicted as the children are."

By May the prisons were so crowded that Governor Phips appointed a Special Court of Oyer and Terminer, and the court, having first sought the advice of the Boston clergy, convened in June. One person—Bridget Bishop—was hanged on June 10. Five more were executed on July 19, five on August 19, and eight on September 22, making a total of nineteen, not counting Giles Corey, who was pressed to death on September 19 for refusing to plead to his indictment.

It is worth noticing Bridget Bishop's special position in this sequence. She was far from the first person accused. She was not examined until April 19, more than a month and a half after the examinations had begun. Yet she was hanged, and hanged alone, on June 10. Sarah Good, who had been examined with Tituba on March 1, the first day of the examinations, was not executed until July 19. The difference is that there was better and more concrete evidence against Bridget Bishop than against Sarah Good.

The Boston clergy had advised the court that they should not put too much weight upon purely "spectral" evidence, that is, upon the appearance of the spectre of an accused person in the hallucinations of the afflicted girls. They knew, like Hamlet, that "the Devil hath power / to assume a pleasing shape." Indeed, as Cotton Mather put it in a letter to one of the judges, "the devils have sometimes represented the shapes of persons not only innocent, but also very virtuous." Unfortunately, some of the most important people at Salem were not of this opinion. The Reverend Samuel Parris of Salem Village, the Reverend Nicholas Noyes of Salem Town, examining magistrates Hathorne and Corwin and Chief Justice Stoughton were all of the opinion that God would not permit the Devil to appear in the shape of an innocent person. They treated spectral evidence throughout as conclusive evidence of guilt. Yet they had been warned not to use it as the sole ground for conviction, and they therefore looked for other evidence. In Bridget Bishop's case they found it, and of a concrete and damning kind: two workmen swore that in taking down the wall of a house where she had lived they found dolls with headless pins stuck in them.

The evidence was circumstantial. But evidence is hard to find in witchcraft cases, since witchcraft is, after all, conducted in secret. Coupled with other testimony, the finding of the dolls was very convincing. I think there is no question that the same evidence would have got Bridget Bishop hanged in England, or burned in Scotland or on the Continent. Indeed, it is extremely probable that Bridget Bishop was a practicing witch. It is possible that, of those who were hanged, the same is true of one or two others, although the evidence in their cases is much less persuasive. But the majority were executed on only two grounds, spectral evidence plus the accumulating weight of the confessions, and there is now no doubt at all that the majority were innocent.

What brought the matter to an end, however, was not the suspicion that some of those executed might have been innocent so much as the astonishing multiplication in the number of those accused, coupled with the fact that as the accusations multiplied they ceased to be directed at persons likely to be witches—persons of known malevolence, or otherwise disreputable. Indeed the accusations finally included persons so obviously virtuous and innocent that nobody could believe them guilty. (Similar circumstances ended the career of the late Senator McCarthy. The nation simply could not believe that all those clean-cut young Army officers were subversive.)

On October 3 the Reverend Increase Mather read his "Cases of Conscience Concerning Evil Spirits Personating Men" to the ministers of Boston, and it was primarily this document that convinced Governor Phips, later in the month, to forbid further arrests or executions. By the end of the month the General Court (the legislature) had dismissed the Special Court of Oyer and Terminer, and called for a fast and the ministers' counsel.

Medical and Psychological Explanations

The early historians of Salem witchcraft had little patience with the argument that the afflicted girls were mentally unbalanced. But as the scientific study of the mind grew to respectability, it became possible to explain the witchcraft outbreak in psychological terms. By the early twentieth century, it was widely accepted that some sort of "hysteria" played a part in the tragedy.

In a 1943 article in the American Journal of Diseases of Children, *ERNEST CAULFIELD (1894–1972), a peditrician and amateur historian, attempted to give some substance to this thesis. He began by analyzing seventeenth century descriptions of the behavior of children who were thought to be bewitched, and paid particular attention to an account by Cotton Mather of a young Boston girl, Martha Goodwin. Caulfield determines that these children were indeed suffering from hysteria, and he proceeds to explain how the precarious mental state of Puritan young people was brought about by the morbid and repressive nature of their upbringing.*

But does Caulfield really come to grips with the vague concept of hysteria? If all Puritan children shared a tendency to hysteria, why is it that the affliction did not erupt in other New England towns as it did in Salem? Conversely, why did equally violent episodes of witch hunting occur in non-Puritan societies where, presumably, childrearing practices were different?

8. A Physician Diagnoses Hysteria

Fortunately, because it is helpful in the diagnosis, there still exists a record of one case of witchcraft in which the fits of some bewitched children are described in great detail. This is called "Memorable Providences, Relating to Witchcraft and Possessions," and chiefly because of its detailed descriptions it is a most valuable contribution to early American medicine, though not hitherto so regarded. This case history of the Goodwin children was written a few years before the Salem tragedy. On the surface, it may seem illogical to use a Boston witchcraft case of 1688 to help explain the Salem cases of 1692,

From Ernest Caulfield, "Pediatric Aspects of the Salem Witchcraft Tragedy," *American Journal of Diseases of Children*, vol. 65 (May 1943), pp. 788–802. Copyright 1943, American Medical Association. Reprinted by permission of the American Medical Association.

but all historians agree on the almost perfect similarity in the cases and my only reason for citing these earlier cases from Boston is that here one finds a connected story limited almost exclusively to a description of the fits. Another objection to using the "Memorable Providences" is that the author, Cotton Mather, is known to have been prejudiced in favor of witchcraft. But strange as it may seem to some, the Puritans, and particularly Cotton Mather, did not oppose, but indeed advanced, the growth of science. It was this same Cotton Mather, member of the Royal Society, who wrote the first American description of measles (which, incidentally, is an American classic), and it was he who, in spite of tremendous opposition from the medical profession, influenced Zabdiel Boylston to try inoculation against smallpox, the first step toward the prevention of diseases. Mather steadfastly maintained in his "Memorable Providences" that he was recording actual facts, and, though considerable allowance should be made for his superstition, gullibility and firm belief in witchcraft, it is clear that the descriptions must have been founded mostly on observations, not only because of the similarity to the Salem court records, with which he had nothing to do, but chiefly because, even after these two hundred and fifty years, one can recognize the sickness that afflicted the Goodwin children as easily as though they had had the smallpox.

The "Memorable Providences" concerns John Goodwin, a mason, and his wife, who with their six children, Nathaniel 15, Martha 13, John 11, Mercy 7 and Benjamin 5 years and Hannah 6 months old, comprised an extremely religious family. Indeed, from some of his devout letters still extant it appears that John Goodwin was the kind of mason who would have said a prayer every time he laid a brick. One day Martha Goodwin accused the family washerwoman of stealing some of the family linen, whereupon the washerwoman's "wild Irish" mother, old Goody Glover, "bestow'd very bad Language upon the Girl . . . immediately upon which, the poor child became variously indisposed in her health, and visited with strange Fits, beyond those that attend an Epilepsy, or a Catalepsy, or those they call The Diseases of Astonishment." Shortly after, John, Mercy and Benjamin began to behave in a strange manner too, though "the godly father and the suckling Infant, were not afflicted" nor was Nathaniel except in slight degree. The most skilful Boston physicians, unable to find any physical cause, concluded that the children were afflicted with "an Hellish Witchcraft," and, needless to say, poor Goody Glover was therefore put to death. Later, Cotton Mather took the afflicted Martha Goodwin into his own home and after many months of observation wrote his account, from which the following passage is taken:

The variety of their tortures increased continually; and tho about Nine or Ten at Night they alwaies had a Release from their miseries, and ate, and slept all night for the most part indifferently well, yet in the day time they were handled with so many sorts of Ails, that it would require of us almost as much time to Relate them all, as it did of them to Endure them. Sometimes they would be Deaf, sometimes Dumb, and sometimes Blind, and often, all this at once. One while their Tongues would be drawn down their Throats; another-while they would be pull'd out upon their Chins, to a prodigious length. They would have their Mouths opened unto such a Wideness, that their Jaws went out of joint; and anon they would clap together again with the Force like that of a strong Spring-Lock. The same would happen to their Shoulder-Blades, and their Elbows, and Hand-wrists, and several of their joints. They would at times ly in a benummed condition; and be drawn together as those that are ty'd Neck and Heels; and presently be stretched out, yea, drawn Backwards, to such a degree that it was fear'd the very skin of their Bellies would have crack'd. They would make most pitteous out-cries, that they were cut with Knives, and struck with Blows that they could not bear. Their necks would be broken, so that their Neck-bone would seem dissolved unto them that felt after it; and yet on the sudden, it would become again so stiff that there was no stirring of their Heads; yea, their Heads would be twisted almost round; and if main force at any time obstructed a dangerous motion which they seem'd to be upon, they would roar exceedingly. . . .

The Fits of the Children yet more arriv'd unto such Motions as were beyond the Efficacy of any natural Distemper in the World. They would bark at one another like Dogs, and again purr like so many Cats. They would sometimes complain, that they were in a Red-hot Oven, sweating and panting at the same time unreasonably: Anon they would say, Cold water was thrown upon them, at which they would shiver very much. They would cry out of dismal Blowes with great Cudgels laid upon them; and tho' we saw no cudgels nor blowes, yet we could see the Marks left by them in Red Streaks upon their bodies afterward. And one of them [John, 11 years old] would be roasted on an invisible Spit, run into his Mouth, and out at his Foot, he lying, and rolling, and groaning as if it had been so in the most sensible manner in the world; and then he would shriek, that Knives were cutting of him. Sometimes also he would have his head so forcibly, tho not visibly, nail'd unto the Floor, that it was as much as a strong man could do to pull it up. One while they would all be so limber, that it was judg'd every Bone of them could be bent. Another while they would be so stiff, that not a joint of them could be stir'd. . . .

Many wayes did the Devils take to make the children do mischief both to themselves and others; but thro the singular Providence of God, they always fail'd in the attempts. For they could never essay the doing of any harm, unless there were some-body at hand that might prevent it; and seldome without first shrieking out, "They say, I must do such a thing!" Diverse times they went to strike furious Blowes at their tenderest and dearest friends, or to fling them down staires when they had them at the top, but the warnings from the mouths of the children themselves, would still anticipate what the Devils did intend. They diverse times were very near Burning or Drowning of themselves, but the children themselves by their own pittiful and seasonale cries for help, still procurred their Deliverance. . . . But if any small Mischief happen'd to be done where they were; as the Tearing or Dirtying of a Garment, the Falling of a Cup, the breaking of a Glass or the like; they would rejoice extremely, and fall into a pleasure and Laughter very extraordinary. . . .

Variety of Tortures now seiz'd upon the Girl [Martha, 13 years old]; in which besides the forementioned Ails returning upon her, she often would cough up a Ball as big as a small Egg, into the side of her Wind-pipe, that would near choak her, till by Stroking and by Drinking it was carried down again. . . .

The Last Fit that the young woman had, was very peculiar. The Daemons having once again seiz'd her, they made her pretend to be Dying, and Dying truly we fear'd at last she was: She lay, she tossed, she pull'd just like one Dying, and urged hard for some to dy with her, seeming loth to dy alone. She argued concerning Death, in strains that quite amazed us; and concluded, That though she was loth to dy, yet if God said she must, she must; adding something about the state of the Country, which we wondered at. Anon, the Fit went over; and as I guessed it would be, it was the last Fit she had at our House.

Inasmuch as old men and women were condemned to death as wizards and witches on this sort of evidence, it is easy to understand the unbridled scorn of the historians; and yet it is important to emphasize that there is enough here, to say nothing of the passages not cited, for an abolute diagnosis. It is also easy to show that the Salem children suffered from hysteria too, for there is hardly a sign or symptom manifested by Martha Goodwin that did not have its counterpart in one or another of the Salem children during their bewitchment. They too made "great noises" during their "lamentable fits and agonies"; they too were "dreadfully tortured" and "struck dumb and senseless for a season"; according to the Rev. Mr. Hale, "Sometimes they were taken dumb, their mouths stopped, their throats choked, their limbs wracked and tormented so as might move an heart of stone." Samuel Sewall, of all the Puritans the most generally successful in keeping his feet on the ground, meant exactly what he said when he wrote in his diary: "It was awful to see the tortures of the afflicted." During the trial of that "rampant hag" Martha Carrier, the afflicted were "so tortured that every one expected their death upon the very spot."

By patching together the sworn testimony of numerous witnesses during the trial of Mary Easty and by making a few minor alterations for the sake of continuity, one can obtain a fairly connected first-hand description of the fits of the Salem children on one occasion at least. At the preliminary hearing in Salem Village during April 1692, five of the afflicted children were "choked in such a most grievous manner" that the examination had to be interrupted, and in spite of the prayers of the Rev. Mr. Hale they remained "almost choked to death." For some now unknown reason Mary Easty was released on May 18. On May 20, Mercy Lewis, a 17 year old servant girl, had a fit in the house of her master, Constable John Putnam.

One man testified:

I went to that house about 9 a clock in the morning and when I came there Mercy Lewis lay on the bed in a sad condition and continued speechless for about an hour. [He then left for a while but came back.] She continued in a sad condition the greatest part of the day being in such tortures as no tongue can express; but not able to speak. But at last she said "Deare Lord Receive my soule" and again said "Lord let them not kill me yett" but at last she came to herself for a little while and was very sensible and then she said that Goody Easty said she would kill her before midnight. . . . Then again presently she felt very bad and cried out "Pray for the salvation of my soule for they will kill me."

Four other men who were in that house between 8 and 11 o'clock that night testified that Elizabeth Hubbard, another 17 year old girl, was brought in while they were there. They found Mercy Lewis "in such a case as if death would have quickly followed . . . being unable to speak most of the day." The two girls then "fell into fits by turns, the one being well whilst the other was ill . . . and [the apparition] vexed and tortured them both by choking and seemingly breathless fits and other fits, threatening Mercy Lewis with a winding sheet & afterwards with a Coffin if said Mercy would not sign the Devil's book. Abundance more of vexations they both received from her [the apparition]."

Still two other men had been at the house that day and found Mercy Lewis in a very Dreadful and Solemn Condition so that Shee could not continue long in this world without a mitigation of those Torments. [They left the house for a while but] Returning the same night aboute midnight, wee found Mercy Lewis in a Dreadful fitt but her reason then Returned Again. She said "What, have you brought me the winding sheet, Goody Easty? Well, I had rather go into the winding sheet than Sett my hand to the Devil's book" but after that her fitts was weaker and weaker but still complaining that Shee was very sick of her stomake. About break of Day She fell asleep but still Continues extreem sick and was taken with a Dreadful fitt just as we left her so that we perceived life in her and that was all.

Another man testified that she was "grievously afflicted and tortured . . . choked allmost to death . . . and we looked for nothing else but present death." Her fit continued well into the next day.

During most of the fit the girl was in a stupor and could not speak; so Ann Putnam (12 years), Abigail Williams (11 years) and Elizabeth Hubbard (17 years) were summoned to the bedside to attempt to identify the apparition that was tormenting Mercy Lewis. The three said that it was the apparition of Goody Easty. Near midnight, when the fit was extra severe, two men rushed out of that haunted house, hastened to Salem for a warrant and then went to Topsfield and dragged Goody Easty out of bed. She was 58 years old and the mother of seven children, yet they took her back to Salem jail and chained her to a cell. She was brought to trial, and, chiefly because of Mercy Lewis' fit and similar evidence, she was convicted and subsequently hanged.

Because of the similarity in the two instances, one could expect that the same historians who have considered the Salem children as "frauds" should have also condemned the Goodwin children as deceitful "pests," they apparently having overlooked the fact that Cotton Mather, like the Salem judges, did consider the possibility of sham but quickly rejected it. Just because some passages in the "Memorable Providences" make it appear as though Martha Goodwin may have had her tongue in her cheek while she was being observed, one can hardly conclude that Cotton Mather's whole account was ludicrous, written in a "style of blind and absurd credulity that cannot be surpassed." That the children's afflictions were attributed to the capital crime of witchcraft is deplorable enough, to say the least, but that is not the point at issue. It is essential to remember that lying was only a symptom and that primarily the children were afflicted with a mental illness. Having studied medicine and probably knowing as much about sickness as any New England physician, Mather deserves a little credit for recognizing that there was at least something unusual about this girl. "But I am resolved after this" he wrote after observing her for many months, "never to use but one grain of patience with any man that shall go to impose upon me a Denial of Devils, or of Witches. I shall count that man Ignorant who shall suspect, but I shall count him down-right Impudent, if he Assert the Non-Existence of things *which we have had such palpable convictions of.*" (The italics are mine).

It therefore seems reasonable to conclude that not the apparent lying but the "extreme agony of all the afflicted" accounts for the decided convictions of the judges, jury and spectators, many of them educated and reasonable men. In some cases "the tortures and lamentations of the afflicted" convinced even the relatives of the accused, and in the trials of Rebecca Nurse and a few others even the accused themselves, though vehemently denying their own guilt, nevertheless admitted that the children acted as though bewitched. Not unimportant is the fact that more than one trial had to be postponed because the children could not possibly be relieved of their "agony" by binding the accused, by prayer or by any other means. And when their trials were over, at least two convicted witches were unaminously excommunicated from the church, a horrible punishment in Puritan times, especially to one about to die. The possibility that the judges were unfair being laid aside for the moment, would the men and women of the church willingly and unaminously convict their intimate friends, whom they knew to be otherwise honorable, except for this very, very convicing evidence of "stupendous Witchcraft?"

Far more fundamental to a true understanding of the Salem tragedy than the diagnosis of hysteria are the factors at play which could have caused so much hysteria among the children of those days: hence, by far the most interesting feature of Mather's account of the Goodwin children is that every now and then he allows a glimpse of the underlying cause. The following quotation is not an isolated passage lifted from its context merely to prove a point but is representative of many similar passages, and consequently the cause and effect sequence seems more than accidental:

But nothing in the World would so discompose them as a Religious Exercise. If there were any Discourse of God, or Christ, or any of the things which are not seen and are eternal, they would be cast into intolerable Anguishes. Once, those two Worthy Ministers, Mr. Fisk and Mr. Thatcher, bestowing some gracious Counsils on the Boy, whom they then found at a Neighbours house, he immediately lost his Hearing, so that he heard not one word, but just the last word of all they said. Much more, All Praying to God, and Reading of his Word, would occasion a very terrible Vexation to them: They would then stop their own Ears with their own Hands; and roar, and shriek; and holla, to drown the Voice of Devotion. Yea, if any one in the Room took up a Bible to look into it, tho the Children could see nothing of it, as being in a croud of Spectators, or having their Faces another way, yet would they be in wonderful Miseries, till the Bible was laid aside. In short, No good thing must be endured near those Children, which (while they are themselves) do love every good thing in a measure that proclaims in them the Fear of God . . . .

Devotion was now, as formerly, the terriblest of all the provocations that could be given her [Martha]. I could by no means bring her to own, That she desired the mercies of God, and the prayers of good men. I would have obtained a Sign of such a Desire, by her Lifting up her hand; but she stirr'd it not: I then lifted up her hand my self, and though the standers-by thought a more insignificant thing could not be propounded. I said, "Child, If you desire those things, let your hand fall, when I take mine away." I took my hand away, and hers continued strangely and stifly stretched out, so that for some time, she could not take it down. During these days we had Prayers oftener in our Family than at other times; and this was her usual Behaviour at them. The man that prayed, usually began with Reading the Word of God; which once as he was going to do, she call'd to him, "Read of Mary Magdalen, out of whom the Lord cast seven Devils." During the time of Reading, she would be laid as one fast asleep; but when Prayer was begun, the Devils would still throw her on the Floor, at the feet of him that prayed. There she would lye and Whistle and sing and roar, to drown the voice of the Prayer; but that being a little too audible for Them, they [the devils] would shut close her Mouth and her ears, and yet make such odd noises in her Throat as that she herself could not hear our Cries to God for her. Shee'd also fetch very terrible Blowes with her Fist, and Kicks with her Foot at the man that pray'd; but still (for he had bid that none should hinder her) her Fist and Foot would alwaies recoil, when they came within a few hairs breadths of him just as if Rebounding against a Wall; so that she touch'd him not, but then would beg hard of other people to strike him, and particularly she entreated them to take the Tongs and smite him; Which not being done, she cryed out of him, "He has wounded me in the Head." But before Prayer was out, she would be laid for Dead, wholly senseless and (unless to a severe Trial) Breathless; with her Belly swelled like a Drum, and sometimes with croaking noises in it; thus would she ly, most exactly with the stiffness and posture of one that had been two Days laid out for Dead. Once lying thus, as he that was praying was alluding to the words of the Canaanites, and saying, "Lord, have mercy on a Daughter, vexed with a Devil; there came a big, but low voice from her, saying, "There's Two or

Three of them'' (or us) and the standers-by were under the Apprehension, as that they cannot relate whether her mouth mov'd in speaking of it. When Prayer was ended, she would Revive in a minute or two, and continue as Frolicksome as before. . . .

Perhaps I have been bewitched into drawing false conclusions, but it seems clear to me that Martha Goodwin had resorted to hysteria mainly because of religious uncertainties and conflicts; and toward a better understanding why Puritan children felt insecure as they contemplated this world and the world hereafter it is now necessary to say something of the Puritan religion. It should go without saying that no sensible man attempts to ridicule any religion so long as it remains a force for good, but, on the other hand, it is important to examine the probable results of the impact of the Puritan religion on the minds of growing children if one wishes to fathom the disastrous events that took place in Salem.

Long before they attained the age of reason, Puritan children were made to learn the contents of John Cotton's catechism, called ''Spiritual Milk for Babes, Drawn out of the Breasts of both Testaments, for their Souls Nourishment.'' Among the first things they learned were the dreadful consequences of Original Sin. All wickedness, all sufferings and diseases, all catastrophes were only manifestations of God's ''Holy Anger'' and ''Holy Jealousy'' because of the fall of Adam and Eve. This doctrine (the sixth question and answer in the catechism) that all children were ''conceived in sin and born in iniquity'' was later carried to its logical conclusion by the preachers of the early eighteenth century. When the Rev. Jabez Fitch found that over 90 per cent of all the deaths from ''throat distemper'' occurred among children, that to him was mathematical proof of the ''woful Effects of Original Sin.'' The brilliant theologian Jonathan Edwards stoutly maintained that sinful children were more hateful than vipers because vipers had no souls. Whitfield literally screamed at his audiences that children were worse than rattlesnakes and alligators, which, he said, were also beautiful when small; and Benjamin Wadsworth said that ''They're Children of Wrath by Nature, liable to Eternal Vengence, the Unquenchable Flames of Hell. . . . Truly it behooves them most seriously to consider how filthy, guilty, odious, and abominable they are both by Nature and Patience.''

There is an illustrative passage in the *Diary of Cotton Mather* dated Nov. 7, 1697:

I took my little [5 year old] daughter, Katy, into my Study, and there I told my child That I am to Dy Shortly and Shee must, when I am Dead, Remember every Thing, that I now said unto her. I sett before her, the sinful . . . condition of her Nature, and I charged her to *pray in secret places every day,* . . . I gave her to understand that when I am taken from her, shee must look to meet with more Humbling Afflictions, than she does.

The literature of colonial times abounds in examples of early piety, instances of "joyful deaths" of children who had learned every word of the catechism, for the Puritans were eager to preserve these instances of holiness in order to impress their remaining children. Cotton Mather has left an account of the precocious Elizabeth Butcher, 2½ years old. "As she lay in the Cradle, she would ask herself that Question, What is my corrupt Nature? and would make Answer to herself, It is empty of Grace, bent into Sin, and only to Sin, and that continually." Many more examples of early piety are related by the Rev. John Brown in his account of "remarkable deaths" during the great diptheria epidemic in Haverhill. Epidemics, catastrophes or deaths of playmates seemed to be opportune occasions to impress on children that they were born under the wrath and curse of God. Here is an interview with a dying 7 year old child:

Being ask'd if she was willing to die, and go to Christ; she said, Yes: But Child you know you are a Sinner; she said Yes: And you know where the Wicked go when they die; she said. Yes they are cast into Hell. And Being asked, if she was not afraid of going thither: she said No, for Christ is an all sufficient Savior, and He is able to save me I hope he will: Tho' I have not yet seen Christ, yet I hope I shall see Him. . . .

A while after she said, I am weary of this World, and long to be gone!

The most pitiful, yet most significant, aspect of this gruesome theology was that the children, once convinced that they were dreadful sinners by birth, could do absolutely nothing about it. There was no use in begging for mercy or forgiveness, because every good Puritan firmly believed in predestination. God, even before the creation of the earth, the sun, the moon and the stars, had already determined who were to be saved and who were to be damned, and no one on earth could be certain whether or not he was among the elect. If God was willing, the adults, by constant prayer and good works, might experience a salvation or a flooding of the soul with an irresistible grace, and with this came the joyful feeling that they were among the elect. But this involved a complex mental process that no child could experience, much less enjoy. And so, with the avenue to mental peace left open only to adults, thoughtful children became terribly bewildered. There are no more pitiful passages in all Puritan literature than those in Sewall's diary wherein he related the gloomy religious outlook of his daughter Betty:

It falls to my [7 year old] daughter Elizabeth's share to read the 24. of Isaiah [which concerns the earth's turning upside down and the inhabitants thereof falling into space] which she doth with many tears not being well and the contents of the chapter and sympathy with her draw tears from me also. . . .

When I came in, past 7. at night, my wife met me in the Entry and told me Betty [13 years old] had surprised them. I was surprised with the abruptness of the Relation. It seems Betty Sewall had given some signs of dejection and sorrow; but a little after dinner she burst out in an amazing cry, which caus'd all the family to cry too; Her mother ask'd the reason; she gave none; at last she said she was afraid she should goe to Hell, her Sins were not pardon'd. She was first wounded by my reading a Sermon of Mr. Norton's, about the 5th of Jan. Text of Jno. 7. 34. Ye shall seek me and shall not find me. And those words in the Sermon Jno. 8. 21. Ye shall seek me and shall die in your sins, ran in her mind and terrified her greatly.

At the age of 16 Nathaniel Mather wrote in his diary: "When very young I went astray from God, and my mind was altogether taken with vanities and follies; such as the remembrance of them doth greatly abase my soul within me. Of the manifold sins which then I was guilty of, none so sticks upon me, as that being very young, I was whittling on the sabbath-day; and for fear of being seen, I did it behind the door. A great reproach of God! a specimen of that atheism that I brought into the world with me." When 19 years old, he confessed on his deathbed that the most bitter of all his trials on earth were "the horrible conceptions of God, buzzing about [his] mind."

It is needless to say much about Puritan conceptions of hell except that epidemics and earthquakes seemed to offer opportune moments for the publication of broadsides and sermons containing the most lurid descriptions. Children were taken on walks through cemeteries to see where other smaller children were buried, for a child was "never too little to die, and never too young to go to hell." The classic example of all this is Michael Wigglesworth's oft-quoted 224 stanza poem on "The Day of Doom" (1662), a work which went through numerous editions and was familiar to nearly every Puritan child. In it are depicted the terrors of the damned in terms that might even today send shivers up the spine of the most confirmed atheistic pediatrician. Of some interest are Wigglesworth's ideas of the punishment inflicted on the newly born, or, as he expressed it, on those who went "from the womb unto the tomb." On the fateful Day of Doom those little infants, exceedingly reluctant to be cast into hell because of Adam's sin, put up a strenuous argument:

> Not we, but he ate of the tree
>   whose fruit was interdicted:
> Yet on us all of his sad fall,
>   the punishment's inflicted.

But all cases were predetermined, so the sentence was nevertheless pronounced:

> You sinners are, and such a share
>   as sinners may expect,
> Such you shall have; for I do save
>   none but my own elect.
> Yet to compare your sin with their
>   who lived a longer time,
> I do confess yours is much less,
>   though every sin's a crime.
> A crime it is, therefore in bliss
>   you may not hope to dwell,
> But unto you I shall allow
>   the easiest room in hell.

Enough has been told to show that the average Puritan child, if he paid any attention to the rigid Calvinism of the times, must have had gloomy prospects of life beyond the grave; and there can be little doubt that some of them at least lived in constant, gnawing fear not only of death but of eternal damnation after death. Thus the appearance of hysteria among the children of Salem Village has an adequate explanation, as it has in the numerous other case histories that are known. Preserved in the Puritan literature are many isolated instances of strange diseases among children which sound much like hysteria. Though perhaps not so dramatic, because there were no executions, but just as important are the examples of mass religious hysteria during the frequent revivals, of which the "Great Awakening" in 1740 is the best example. And it is a curious fact that no one ever blames the children for the outbreak of hysteria at Northampton in 1740, yet the children of Salem are held responsible for what was an essentially similar affair. With a knowledge of the religious background of the Salem children it seems rather unimportant to argue whether Cotton Mather was guilty of the witchcraft hangings by influencing the governor, the judges or the mob on Gallows Hill. He was guilty only insofar as he was a Calvinist; but so, indeed, was nearly everybody else.

The history of the Salem witchcraft should be more concerned with the family background and medical history of the afflicted children, for they were victims as well as the persons who were hanged. It was no coincidence that Martha Goodwin, child of devout parents, acquired her hysteria just at the time when "she was in the dark concerning her Souls estate" and the mere sight of the Bible or the catechism always sent her into "hideous convulsions." Nor was it very strange that the first cases in Salem Village occurred in the very home of the red-hot Devil-chaser, the Rev.Samuel Parris. "Pray for the salvation of my soule for they will kill me," from the mouth of the bewitched Mercy Lewis, was one of the most significant remarks made during the Salem trials. Those children had ample reason to become hysterical when repeatedly told that the monstrous, invisible, venomous, hissing and sooty Devil was right in their neighborhood ready to devour them; and no doubt many of them were positively convinced that they were actually bewitched.

One is not obliged to accept the verdict of the popular historians that the children were deceitful, wicked, malicious and dishonest. History has been unkind to them along enough. They were not imposters or pests or frauds; they were not cold-blooded malignant brats. They were sick children in the worst sort of mental distress—living in fear for their very lives and the welfare of their immortal souls. Hysteria was only the outward manifestation of their feeble attempts to escape from their insecure, cruel, depressive Salem Village world—a world thoroughly saturated with the pungent fumes of burning brimstone.

Is there a physiological explanation for Salem? LINNDA R. CAPORAEL, a young graduate student in biology at the University of California, Santa Barbara, attributed the bizarre behavior of the residents of the village to a disease that is contracted from contaminated grain. The strange fits and visions they experienced were symptoms of this disease, convulsive ergotism.

If true, Caporael's thesis provides a dramatic scientific explanation to an old mystery, and it has the added appeal of linking Salem to the modern drug culture. It was undoubtedly this dramatic quality that motivated the New York Times to announce in a front page article "Salem Witch Hunts in 1692 Linked to LSD-Like Agent."

9. A Biologist Diagnoses Disease

Ergot

Interest in ergot (*Claviceps purpura*) was generated by epidemics of ergotism that periodically occurred in Europe. Only a few years before the Salem witchcraft trials the first medical scientific report on ergot was made. Denis Dodart reported the relation between ergotized rye and bread poisoning

From Linnda R. Caporael, "Ergotism: The Satan Loosed in Salem?" *Science,* vol. 192 (2 April 1976), pp. 21–26. Copyright © 1976 by the American Association for the Advancement of Science. Reprinted by permission of *Science* magazine and the author. Footnotes omitted.

in a letter to the French Royal Academie des Sciences in 1676. John Ray's mention of ergot in 1677 was the first in English. There is no reference to ergot in the United States before an 1807 letter by Dr. John Stearns recommending powdered ergot sclerotia to a medical colleague as a therapeutic agent in childbirth. Stearns is generally credited with the "discovery" of ergot: certainly his use prompted scientific research on the substance. Until the mid-19th century, however, ergot was not known as a parasitic fungus, but was thought to be sunbaked kernels of grains.

Ergot grows on a large variety of cereal grains—especially rye—in a slightly curved, fusiform shape with sclerotia replacing individual grains on the host plant. The sclerotia contain a large number of potent pharmacologic agents, the ergot alkaloids. One of the most powerful is isoergine (lysergic acid amide). This alkaloid, with 10 percent of the activity of D-LSD (lysergic acid diethylamide), is also found in ololiuqui (morning glory seeds), the ritual hallucinogenic drug used by the Aztecs.

Warm, damp, rainy springs and summers favor ergot infestation. Summer rye is more prone to the development of the sclerotia than winter rye, and one field may be heavily ergotized while the adjacent field is not. The fungus may dangerously parasitize a crop one year and not reappear again for many years. Contamination of the grain may occur in varying concentrations. Modern agriculturalists advise farmers not to feed their cattle grain containing more than one to three sclerotia per thousand kernels of grain, since ergot has deleterious effects on cattle as well as on humans.

Ergotism, or long-term ergot poisoning, was once a common condition resulting from eating contaminated rye bread. In some epidemics it appears that females were more liable to the disease than males. Children and pregnant women are most likely to be affected by the condition, and individual susceptibility varies widely. It takes two years for ergot in powdered form to reach 50 percent deterioration, and the effects are cumulative. There are two types of ergotism—gangrenous and convulsive. As the name implies, gangrenous ergotism is characterized by dry gangrene of the extremities followed by the falling away of the affected portions of the body. The condition occurred in epidemic proportions in the Middle Ages and was known by a number of names, including *ignis sacer,* the holy fire.

Convulsive ergotism is characterized by a number of symptoms. These include crawling sensations in the skin, tingling in the fingers, vertigo, tinnitus aurium, headaches, disturbances in sensation, hallucination, painful muscuilar contractions leading to epileptiform convulsions, vomiting, and diarrhea. The involuntary muscular fibers such as the myocardium and gastric and intestinal muscular coat are stimulated. There are mental disturbances such as mania, melancholia, psychosis, and delirium. All of these symptoms are alluded to in the Salem witchcraft records.

Evidence for Ergotism in Salem

It is one thing to suggest convulsive ergot poisoning as an initiating factor in the witchcraft episode, and quite another to generate convicing evidence that it is more than a mere possibility. A jigsaw of details pertinent to growing conditions, the timing of events in Salem, and symptomology must fit together to create a reasonable case. From these details, a picture emerges of a community stricken with an unrecognized physiological disorder affecting their minds as well as their bodies.

1) *Growing conditions.* The common grass along the Atlantic Coast from Virginia to Newfoundland was and is wild rye, a host plant for ergot. Early colonists were dissatisfied with it as forage for their cattle and reported that it often made the cattle ill with unknown diseases. Presumably, then, ergot grew in the New World before the Puritans arrived. The potential source for infection was already present, regardless of the possibility that it was imported with English rye.

Rye was the most reliable of the Old World grains and by the 1640's it was a well-established New England crop. Spring sowing was the rule: the bitter winters made fall sowing less successful. Seed time for the rye was April and the harvesting took place in August. However, the grain was stored in barns and often waited months before being threshed when the weather turned cold. The timing of Salem events fits this cycle. Threshing probably occurred shortly before Thanksgiving, the only holiday the Puritans observed. The children's symptoms appeared in December 1691. Late the next fall, 1692, the witchcraft crisis ended abruptly and there is no further mention of the girls or anyone else in Salem being afflicted.

To some degree or another all rye was probably infected with ergot. It is a matter of the extent of infection and the period of time over which the ergot is consumed rather than the mere existence of ergot that determines the potential for ergotism. In his 1807 letter written from upstate New York. Stearns advised his medical colleague that, "On examining a granary where rye is stored, you will be able to procure a sufficient quantity [of ergot sclerotia] from among that grain." Agricultural practice had not advanced, even by Stearns's time, to widespread use of methods to clean or eliminate the fungus from the rye crop. In all probability, the infestation of the 1691 summer rye crop was fairly light; not everyone in the village or even in the same families showed symptoms.

Certain climatic conditions, that is, warm, rainy springs and summers, promote heavier than usual fungus infestation. The pattern of the weather in 1691 and 1692 is apparent from brief comments in Samuel Sewall's diary. Early rains and warm weather in the spring progressed to a hot and stormy summer in 1691. There was a drought the next year, 1692, thus no contamination of the grain that year would be expected.

2) *Localization*. "Rye," continues Stearns "which grows in low, wet ground yields [ergot] in greatest abundance." Now, one of the most notorious of the accusing children in Salem was Thomas Putnam's 12-year-old daughter, Ann. Her mother also displayed symptoms of the affliction and psychological historians have credited the senior Ann with attempting to resolve her own neurotic complaints through her daughter. Two other afflicted girls also lived in the Putnam residence. Putnam had inherited one of the largest landholdings in the village. His father's will indicates that a large measure of the land, which was located in the western sector of Salem Village, consisted of swampy meadows that were valued farmland to the colonists. Accordingly, the Putnam farm, and more broadly, the western acreage of Salem Village, may have been an area of contamination. This contention is further substantiated by the pattern of residence of the accusers, the accused, and the defenders of the accused living within the boundaries of Salem Village. Excluding the afflicted girls, 30 of 32 adult accusers lived in the western section and 12 of the 14 accused witches lived in the eastern section, as did 24 of the 29 defenders. The general pattern of residence, in combination with the well-documented factionalism of the eastern and western sectors, contributed to the progress of the witchcraft crisis.

The initially afflicted girls show a slightly different residence pattern. Careful examination reveals plausible explanations for contamination in six of the eight cases.

Three of the girls, as mentioned above, lived in the Putnam residence. If this were the source of ergotism, their exposure to ergotized grain would be natural. Two afflicted girls, the daughter and niece of Samuel Parris, lived in the parsonage almost exactly in the center of the village. Their exposure to contaminated grain from western land is also explicable. Two-thirds of Parris' salary was paid in provisions; the villagers were taxed proportionately to their landholding. Since Putnam was one of the largest landholders and an avid supporter of Parris in the minister's community disagreements, an ample store of ergotized grain would be anticipated in Parris's larder. Putnam was also Parris's closest neighbor with afflicted children in residence.

The three remaining afflicted girls lived outside the village boundaries to the east. One, Elizabeth Hubbard, was a servant in the home of Dr. Griggs. It seems plausible that the doctor, like Parris, had Putnam grain, since Griggs was a professional man, not a farmer. As the only doctor in town, he probably had many occasions to treat Ann Putnam, Sr., a woman known to have much ill health. Griggs may have traded his services for provisions or bought food from the Putnams.

Another of the afflicted, Sarah Churchill, was a servant in the house of a well-off farmer. The farm lay along the Wooleston River and may have offered good growing conditions for ergot. It seems probable, however, that Sarah's affliction was a fraud. She did not become involved in the witchcraft persecutions until May, several months after the other girls were afflicted, and she testified in only two cases, the first against her master. One deponent claimed that Sarah later admitted to belying herself and others.

How Mary Warren, a servant in the Proctor household, would gain access to grain contaminated with ergot is something of a mystery. Proctor had a substantial farm to the southeast of Salem and would have had no need to buy or trade for food. Both he and his wife were accused of witchcraft and condemned. None of the Proctor children showed any sign of the affliction; in fact, three were accused and inprisoned. One document offered as evidence against Proctor indicates that Mary stayed overnight in the village. How often she stayed or with whom is unknown.

Mary's role in the trials is particularly curious. She began as an afflicted person, was accused of witchcraft by the other afflicted girls, and then became afflicted again. Two depositions filed against her strongly suggest, however, that at least her first affliction may have been a consequence of ergot poisoning. Four witnesses attested that she believed she had been "distempered" and during the time of her affliction had thought she had seen numerous apparitions. However, when Mary was well again, she could not say that she had seen any specters. Her second affliction may have been the result of intense pressure during her examination for witchcraft crimes.

Ergotism and the Testimony

The utmost caution is necessary in assessing the physical and mental states of people dead for hundreds of years. Only the sketchiest accounts of their lives remain in public records. In the case of ergot, a substance that affects mental as well as physical states, recognition of the social atmosphere of Salem in early spring 1692 is basic to understanding the directions the crisis took. The Puritans' belief in witchcraft was a totally accepted part of their religious tenets. The malicious workings of Satan and his cohorts were just as real to the early colonists as their belief in God. Yet, the low incidence of witchcraft trials in New England prior to 1692 suggests that the Puritans did not always resort to accusations of black magic to deal with irreconcilable differences or inexplicable events.

The afflicted girls' behavior seemed to be no secret in early spring. Apparently it was the great consternaton that some villagers felt that induced Mary Sibley to direct the making of the witch cake of rye meal and the urine of the afflicted. This concoction was fed to a dog, ostensibly in the belief that the dog's subsequent behavior would indicate the action of any malefic magic. The fate of the dog is unknown; it is quite plausible that it did have convulsions, indicating to the observers that there was witchcraft involved in the girls' afflictions. Thus, the experiments with the witch cake, rather than any magic tricks by Tituba, initiated succeeding events.

The importance of the witch cake incident has generally been overlooked. Parris's denouncement of his neighbor's action is recorded in his church records. He clearly stated that, until the making of the cake, there was no suspicion of witchcraft and no reports of torturing apparitions. Once a community member had gone "to the Devil for help against the Devil," as Parris put it, the climate for the trials had been established. The afflicted girls, who had made no previous mention of witchcraft, seized upon a cause for their behavior—as did the rest of the community. The girls named three persons as witches and their afflictions thereby became a matter for the legal authorities rather than the medical authorities or the families of the girls.

The trial records indicate numerous interruptions during the proceedings. Outbursts by the afflicted girls describing the activities of invisible specters and "familiars" (agents of the devil in animal form) in the meeting house were common. The girls were often stricken with violent fits that were attributed to torture by apparitions. The spectral evidence of the trials appears to be the hallucinogenic symptoms and perceptual disturbances accompanying ergotism. The convulsions appear to be epileptiform.

Accusations of choking, pinching, pricking with pins, and biting by the specter of the accused formed the standard testimony of the afflicted in almost all the examinations and trials. The choking suggests the involvement of the involuntary muscular fibers that is typical of ergot poisoning; the biting, pinching, and pricking may allude to the crawling and tingling sensations under the skin experienced by ergotism victims. Complaints of vomiting and "bowels almost pulled out" are common in the depositions of the accusers. The physical symptoms of the afflicted and many of the other accusers are those induced by convulsive ergot poisoning.

When examined in the light of a physiological hypothesis, the content of so-called delusional testimony, previously dismissed as imaginary by historians, can be reinterpreted as evidence of ergotism. After being choked and strangled by the apparition of a witch sitting on his chest, John Londer testified that a black thing came through the window and stood before his face. "The body of it looked like a monkey, only the feet were like cock's feet, with claws, and the face somewhat more like a man's than a monkey . . . the thing spoke to me. . .''

Joseph Bayley lived out of town in Newbury. According to Upham, the Bayleys, en route to Boston, probably spent the night at the Thomas Putnam residence. As the Bayleys left the village, they passed the Proctor house and Joseph reported receiving a "very hard blow" on the chest, but no one was near him. He saw the Proctors, who were imprisoned in Boston at the time, but his wife told him that she saw only a "little maid." He received another blow on the chest, so strong that he dismounted from his horse and subsequently saw a woman coming toward him. His wife told him she saw nothing. When he mounted his horse again, he saw only a cow where he had seen the woman. The rest of Bayley's trip was uneventful, but when he returned home, he was "pinched and nipped by something invisible for some time." It is a moot point, of course, what or how much Bayley ate at the Putnams', or that he even really stayed there. Nevertheless, the testimony suggests ergot. Bayley had the crawling sensations in the skin, disturbances in sensations, and muscular contractions symptomatic of ergotism. Apparently his wife had none of the symptoms and Bayley was quite candid in so reporting.

A brief but tantalizing bit of testimony comes from a man who experienced visions that he attributed to the evil eye cast on him by an accused witch. He reported seeing about a dozen "strange things" appear in his chimney in a dark room. They appeared to be something like jelly and quavered with a strange motion. Shortly, they disappeared and a light the size of a hand appeared in the chimney and quivered and shook with an upward motion. As in Bayley's experience, this man's wife saw nothing. The testimony is strongly reminiscent of the undulating objects and lights reported in experience induced by LSD.

By the time the witchcraft episode ended in the late fall 1692, 20 persons had been executed and at least two had died in prison. All the convictions were obtained on the basis of the controversial spectral evidence. One of the commonly expressed observations about the Salem Village witchcraft episode is that it ended unexpectedly for no apparent reason. No new circumstances to cast spectral evidence in doubt occurred. Increase Mather's sermon on 3 October 1692, which urged more conclusive evidence than invisible apparitions or the test of touch, was just a stronger reiteration of the clergy's

15 June advice to the court. The grounds for dismissing the spectral evidence had been consistently brought up by the accused and many of their defenders throughout the examinations. There had always been a strong undercurrent of opposition to the trials and the most vocal individuals were not always accused. In fact, there was virtually no support in the colonies for the trials, even from Boston, only 15 miles away. The most influential clergymen lent their support guardedly at best; most were opposed. The Salem witchcraft episode was an event localized in both time and space.

How far the ergotized grain may have been distributed is impossible to determine clearly. Salem Village was the source of Salem Town's food supply. It was in the town that the convictions and orders for executions were obtained. Maybe the thought processes of the magistrates, responsible and respected men in the Colony, were altered. In the following years, nearly all of them publicly admitted to errors of judgment. These posttrial documents are as suggestive as the court proceedings.

In 1696, Samuel Sewall made a public acknowledgment of personal guilt because of the unsafe principles the court followed. In a public apology, the 12 jurymen stated, "We confess that we ourselves were not capable to understand nor able to withstand the mysterious delusion of the Powers of Darkness and Prince of the Air . . . [we] do hereby declare that we justly fear that we were sadly deluded and mistaken. . ." John Hale, a minister involved in the trials from the beginning, wrote: "such was the darkness of the day . . . that we walked in the clouds and could not see our way."

Finally, Ann Putnam, Jr., who testified in 21 cases, made a public confession in 1706.

> I justly fear I have been instrumental with others though ignorantly and unwittingly, to bring upon myself and this land the guilt of innocent blood; though what was said or done by me against any person I can truly and uprightly say before God and man, I did it not for any anger, malice or ill will to any person for I had no such things against one of them, but what I did was ignorantly, being deluded of Satan.

One Satan in Salem may well have been convulsive ergotism.

Conclusion

One could reasonably ask whether, if ergot was implicated in Salem, it could have been implicated in other witchcraft incidents. The most cursory examination of Old World witchcraft suggests an affirmative answer. The district of Lorraine suffered outbreaks of both ergotism and witchcraft persecutions throughout the Middle Ages until the 17th century. As late as the 1700's, the clergy of Saxony debated whether convulsive ergotism was symptomatic of disease or demonic possession. Kittredge, an authority on English witchcraft reports what he calls "a typical case" of the 1600's. The malicious magic of Alice Trevisard, an accused witch, backfired and the witness reported that Alice's hands, fingers, and toes "rotted and consumed away." The sickness sounds suspiciously like gangrenous ergotism. Years later, in 1762, one family in a small English village was stricken with gangrenous ergotism. The Royal Society determined the diagnosis. The head of the family, however, attributed the condition to witchcraft because of the suddenness of the calamity.

Of course, there can never be hard proof for the presence of ergot in Salem, but a circumstantial case is demonstrable. The growing conditions and the pattern of agricultural practices fit the timing of the 1692 crisis. The physical manifestations of the condition are apparent from the trial records and contemporaneous documents. While the fact of perceptual distortions may have been generated by ergotism, other psychological and sociological factors are not thereby rendered irrelevant; rather, these factors gave substance and meaning to the symptoms. The content of hallucinations and other perceptual disturbances would have been greatly influenced by the state of mind, mood, and expectations of the individual. Prior to the witch cake episode, there is no clue as to the nature of the girls' hallucinations. Afterward, however, a delusional system, based on witchcraft, was generated to explain the content of the sensory data. Valins and Nisbett, in a discussion of delusional explanations of abnormal sensory data, write, "The intelligence of the particular patient determines the structural coherence and internal consistency of the explanation. The cultural experiences of the patient determine the content—political, religious, or scientific—of the explanation." Without knowledge of ergotism and confronted by convulsions, mental disturbances, and perceptual distortions, the New England Puritans seized upon witchcraft as the best explanation for the phenomena.

Two psychologists at Carleton University, NICHOLAS P. SPANOS (b. 1942) and JACK GOTTLIEB (b.1951), have challenged Linnda Caporael's thesis that ergot poisoning lay at the basis of the witchcraft outbreak. In an article published in Science *magazine, Spanos and Gottlieb argue that most of the symptoms of ergotism were not exhibited at Salem. The fact that the fits and visions of the witnesses seemed to start and stop on cue suggests a social, rather than a physiological explanation.*

This is an interesting example of how researchers working with the same source material can arrive at strikingly different conclusions. It remains for the reader to decide which of the two interpretations is most persuasive.

10. The Disease Diagnosis Disputed

In a recent article in *Science* it was suggested that the residents of Salem Village, Massachusetts, who in 1692 charged some of their neighbors with witchcraft did so because of delusions resulting from convulsive ergotism. The author of the article, L. R.Caporael, argued that (i) the general features of the Salem crisis corresponded to the features of an epidemic of convulsive ergotism, (ii) syptoms manifested by the girls who were the principal accusers were those of ergot poisoning, (iii) the symptoms shown by the other accusing witnesses were also those of convulsive ergotism, and (iv) the abrupt ending of the Salem crisis suggests ergot poisoning. We shall attempt to show that these arguments are not well founded.

Features of Convulsive Ergotism Epidemics

Ergot is a fungus (*Claviceps purpurea*) that under some conditions infests rye and other cereal grains. When ingested the ergotized grain may produce a variety of cardiovascular effects leading, among other things, to gangrene (gangrenous ergotism), or neurological effects leading, among other things, to convulsions (convulsive ergotism). Epidemics of convulsive ergotism have a number of general features that differ substantially from the events that occurred in Salem.

According to Barger, epidemics of convulsive ergotism have occurred almost exclusively in locales where the inhabitants suffered severe vitamin A deficiencies. Ergot poisoning in individuals with adequate vitamin A intakes

From Nicholas P. Spanos and Jack Gottlieb, "Ergotism and the Salem Village Witch Trials," *Science*, vol. 194 (24 December 1976), pp. 1390–1394. Copyright © 1976 by the American Association for the Advancement of Science. Reprinted by permission of *Science* magazine and the authors. Footnotes omitted.

leads to gangrenous rather than convulsive symptoms. Vitamin A is found both in fish and in dairy products. Salem Village was a farming community and Salem Town, which bordered the village, was a well-known seaport; cows and fish were plentiful. There is no evidence to suggest a vitamin A deficiency in the diet of the inhabitants, and it would be particularly unlikely for the so-called "afflicted girls," some of whom came from well-to-do farming families. The absence of any instance of gangrenous symptomatology makes it highly unlikely that ergot played any role in the Salem crisis.

Young children are particularly susceptible to convulsive ergotism. Barger states:

> All accounts of convulsive ergotism agree that children were more liable to convulsive ergotism than adults; thus 56 percent in the Finnish epidemic were under 10 years of age; 60 percent of Scrinc's cases were under 15 years of age. . .

Only 3 of the 11 afflicted girls in Salem were under 15 years of age and only one of those was under 10. There is no evidence either in the trial records or in eyewitness accounts to indicate a high rate of convulsive symptoms in the young children of Salem Village during the witch crisis. In fact we could find references to only two cases of convulsions in children under ten during the period of the crisis. One of these was the afflicted girl mentioned above. The other was an 8-week-old infant that convulsed before it died. An 8-week-old infant would not yet have been weaned, and nursing infants do not suffer ergot poisoning even if their mothers have a very severe case of the disease; it is therefore unlikely that this infant died from ergotism.

The fact that most of the individuals (including young children) living in the same households as the afflicted girls showed no symptoms is attributed by Caporael to wide indiviual differences in susceptibility to ergot poisoning. While there are wide individual differences in susceptibility to gangrenous ergotism, convulsive ergotism is another matter. According to Barger it was common for all members of a family to develop symptoms of convulsive ergotism during epidemics. This tendency was so pronounced that convulsive ergotism was long (but erroneously) thought to be infectious.

Convulsive ergotism characteristically produces the following symptoms: (i) vomiting, (ii) diarrhea, (iii) a livid skin color, (iv) sensations of heat and cold in the extremities, (v) spastic muscular contractions in the extremities, which in severe cases may become permanent sequelae, (vi) severe itching and tingling sensations, (vii) convulsions, (viii) a ravenous appetite following convulsions, (ix) death in severe cases. Permanent dementia may also be a symptom in severe cases. Perceptual disturbances may occur, but such disturbances would not be expected to occur independently of the other symptoms.

Caporael says that "complaints of vomiting and 'bowels almost pulled out' are common in the depositions of the accusers." This statement is incorrect. *Records of Salem Witchcraft* (RSW) contains 117 depositions by the afflicted girls and 79 depositions in which other witnesses describe the behaviour of the girls. There are also eyewitness accounts by Mather, Lawson, Brattle, and Hale which are not contained in RSW. We examined all these sources and were unable to find any reference to the occurrence of vomiting or diarrhea among the afflicted girls. In all these sources we found only three instances of gastrointestinal complaints among the girls. In one of these cases the girl making the complaint (Mary Warren) lived outside the area that Caporael suggested was exposed to ergot. Thus 8 of the 11 afflicted girls did not report any gastrointestinal symptoms. Those who did reported only a single instance. None of them reported vomiting or was observed to vomit, and there is no indication that any of them suffered from diarrhea.

We found no indication in any of the works examined that the afflicted girls manifested a livid color of the skin. We found no reference to cold sensations in the extremities, and only two references to burning sensations. In one of those cases an afflicted girl slowly reached out and touched the hood of an accused witch, then immediately pulled back her hand and "cried out, her fingers, her fingers burned." In the second case the judges had obtained a rag puppet which they believed had been used by a witch to afflict people at a distance. They burned the puppet in the presence of the afflicted girls with the following results: "A bit of one of the rags being set on fire (the afflicted) cried out dreadfully (that they were burned)." Rather than ergot poisoning, these descriptions suggest that the afflicted girls were enacting the roles that would sustain their definition of themselves as bewitched and that would lead to the conviction of the accused.

According to Caporael, the afflicted girls' convulsions "appear to be epileptiform" and their reports of being bitten, pinched, and pricked by specters "may allude to the crawling and tingling sensations under the skin experienced by ergotism victims." There is no question that the girls frequently convulsed and reported being bitten and pinched. However, a careful look at the social context in which these symptoms were typically manifested belies the notion that they resulted from an internal disease process. The trial testimony indicates very clearly that the girls convulsed and reported being bitten and pinched when an accused person's behavior provided them with a social cue for such acts.

For example, when one of the accused was ordered to look at an afflicted girl, ''he looked back and knocked down all (or most) of the afflicted who stood behind him.'' In another case, ''As soon as she [the accused witch] came near all [the afflicted] fell into fits.'' The courtroom testimony contains a great many instances of the afflicted girls' convulsing en masse when the accused entered the room, looked in their direction, moved his chair, and so on. The afflicted girls' reports of being pinched, choked, and bitten are described thus by Lawson, an eyewitness:

> It was observed several times, that if she [the accused witch] did but bite her underlip in time of examination the persons afflicted were bitten on their arms and wrists and produced the marks before the magistrates, ministers and others.

The afflicted also produced the pins with which the accused purportedly pinched them.

The afflicted girls were responsive to social cues from each other as well as from the accused and were therefore able to predict the occurrence of each other's fits. In such cases one of the girls would cry out that she saw the specter of an accused witch about to attack another of the afflicted. The other girl would then immediately fall into a fit. Termination of the girls' convulsions was also cued by social-psychological factors. In some cases convulsions would cease when a certain Biblical passage was read. More commonly the girl's convulsions would cease as soon as they were touched by the accused.

Convulsions at the sight of a witch, alleviation of convulsions by the witch's touch, prediction of their own and others' convulsions, and production by the afflicted of bite marks and the pins used to pinch them were all considered standard symptoms in 16th and 17th century cases of demonic possession. Taken together, these facts indicate that the afflicted girls were enacting the role of demoniacs as that role was commonly understood in their day.

Caporael points out that one ergot alkaloid, isoergine (lysergic acid amide), has 10 percent of the activity of LSD and might therefore produce perceptual disturbances. She remarks that ''the spectral evidence of the trials appears to be hallucinogenic symptoms and perceptual disturbances accompanying ergotism.'' The term ''hallucination'' is, unfortunately, very unspecific, and in the psychological literature is used to refer to a wide variety of distinct experiences. Although LSD is commonly referred to as a hallucinogen, Barber has correctly pointed out that ''subjects who have ingested [LSD] very rarely report, when their eyes are open, that they perceive formed persons or objects which they believe are actually out there.'' Instead, they tend to report perceptual distortion such as persistent after-images, rainbow-like colors, halos on the edges of objects, changes in depth perception, contours that appear to undulate, and the like. None of the testimony given by the afflicted girls indicates perceptual distortions of that kind. Instead, they reported seeing "formed persons"—the specters of the accused—attacking, biting, pinching, and choking them and others.

As to the remaining symptoms of ergot poisoning, none of the work we studied indicates that the girls experienced ravenous appetites after their convulsions, suffered permanent contractures of the hands or feet or other signs of permanent neurological damage, suffered permanent dementia, or died. It should be noted that the girls often appeared to be quite healthy outside the courtroom. Even in the courtroom they did not exhibit the signs of chronic malaise and debilitation that might be expected after months of chronic poisoning. Thus, Brattle wrote:

> Many of these afflicted persons, who have scores of strange fits in a day, yet in the intervals of time are hale and hearty, robust and lusty, as tho' nothing had afflicted them. I remember that when the chief Judge gave the first Jury their charge, he told them, that they were not to mind whether the bodies of the said afflicted were really pined and consumed, as was expressed in the indictment; but whether the said afflicted did not suffer from the accused such afflictions as naturally *tended* to their being pined and consumed, wasted etc.

In summary, while the afflicted girls exhibited rather dramatic behavior, none of them displayed the syndrome of convulsive ergotism. Instead, they showed symptoms of "demonic possession," a phenomenon that was fairly common among 16th- and 17th-century Puritans in both England and Colonial America.

It is worth noting that the initial symptoms of the afflicted girls were rather ambiguous, and that they began to correspond more closely to popular stereotypes of demonic behavior as the girls gained increasing exposure to information about those stereotypes. The initial symptoms included "getting into holes, and creeping under chairs and stools, and [using] sundry odd postures and antic gestures, uttering foolish and ridiculous speeches." About 2 weeks after these symptoms began a neighbor had a "witch cake" baked in order to determine whether the girls were bewitched. Only after this event did the girls begin convulsing and reporting the specters of witches. As the witchcraft trials progressed, the girls added to the repertoire. They collapsed en masse when looked at by the accused during the first trial. During the fourth examination they began complaining of being bitten whenever they observed the accused nervously bite her lip and of being pinched when she moved her hand. In later examinations they began to mimic the accused; they held their heads in the same position as that of the accused and rolled their eyes up after the accused did so. This temporal pattern suggests that the demonic manifestations were learned, that the girls' behavior was gradually (although perhaps unwittingly) shaped to fit the expectations for demonic behavior held by the community.

In Caporael's view, there is a "major difficulty in accepting the explanation of purposeful fraud . . . [namely] the gravity of the girls' symptoms." The implication of this statement is that the girls' performances somehow transcended the volitional capacities of normal, physically healthy people. Therefore it should be pointed out that numerous 16th-century English demoniacs who displayed all the symptoms manifested by the Salem girls later confessed that they had faked these displays. They confirmed their confessions by publicly enacting all of their supposedly involuntary symptoms. These facts certainly do not prove that the performances of the Salem girls consisted entirely of conscious faking, but they do indicate that the girls' behavior can be accounted for without recourse to explanations based on unusual diseases.

Symptoms of Other Witnesses

Twenty-nine of the accused witches lived in or on the fringes of Salem Village or had moved from the village within a few years of the crisis. Boyer and Nissenbaum have pointed out that most of the accused lived in one half of the village and most of the witnesses who testified against them lived in the other half. They hypothesize that this geographical split in the pattern of accusations was to a large extent a function of political and social factionalism within the village. Caporael postulates that the accusing witnesses were exposed to ergot poisoning by their location while the accused were not exposed by theirs. She suggests that not only the girls but "many of the other accusers" had physical symptoms such as are "induced by convulsive ergot poisoning."

Records of Salem Witchcraft contains 111 depositions made by 80 different witnesses (not including the afflicted girls) against the 29 accused village residents. Trial records compiled by Boyer and Nissenbaum include a deposition made by one of these witnesses that is not included in RSW. We examined these 112 deposition looking for behavior that, even in a broad sense, might possibly represent symptoms of convulsive ergotism. These symptoms, and the number of individuals who suffered from them, are shown in Table 1. Witnesses were excluded from this table if they reported that their symptoms occurred a year or more before the Salem crisis began (five cases),

Table 1. Symptoms of witnesses (other than the afflicted girls) who testified against the accused witches. A, vomiting. B, diarrhea. C, livid skin. D, permanent contractures. E, pain in extremities. F, death. G, temporary muscle stiffness. H, convulsions. I, ravenous appetite. J, perceptual disturbances (not including apparitions). K, apparitions. L, temporary inability to speak. M, skin sensations of hot and cold. N, skin sensations (biting and pinching). O, choking sensations. P, stomach pain. 1, symptom reported; 0, symptom not reported; ?, symptom questionable.

Reported sufferers	A	B	C	D	E	F	G	H	I	J	K	L	M	N	O	P	Total
W. Allan	0	0	0	0	0	0	0	0	0	0	1	0	0	0	0	0	1
J. Bayley	0	0	0	0	0	0	0	0	0	0	1	0	1	1	0	1	4
S. Bittford	0	0	0	0	0	0	1	0	0	0	1	0	0	0	0	0	2
A. Booth	0	0	0	0	0	0	0	0	0	0	1	0	0	0	0	0	1
J. Childen	0	0	0	0	0	0	0	0	0	0	1	0	0	0	0	0	1
G. Cory	0	0	0	0	0	0	0	?	0	0	0	0	0	0	0	0	1
J. Doritch	0	0	0	0	1	0	0	0	0	0	1	0	1	0	0	0	3
B. Gould	0	0	0	0	0	0	0	?	0	?	1	0	0	0	0	0	3
J. Holton	0	0	0	0	0	0	0	0	0	0	1	0	0	0	0	0	1
J. Hughes	0	0	0	0	0	0	0	1	0	0	0	0	0	0	0	0	1
J. Indian	0	0	0	0	0	0	0	?	0	0	1	0	0	0	0	0	2
T. Indian	0	0	0	0	0	0	0	1	0	0	1	0	0	0	0	0	2
E. Keysar	0	0	0	0	0	0	0	?	0	0	1	0	0	0	0	0	2
M. Pope	0	0	0	0	0	0	0	1	0	0	1	0	0	1	0	0	3
H. Putnam	0	0	0	0	0	0	0	0	0	0	1	0	0	0	0	0	1
J. Putnam	0	0	0	0	0	1	0	0	0	0	0	0	0	0	0	0	1
W. Putnam	0	0	0	0	0	0	1	0	0	0	0	0	0	0	0	0	1
D. Wilkins	0	0	0	0	0	0	0	0	0	0	1	0	0	0	1	0	2
R. Wilkins	0	0	0	0	0	0	0	0	0	0	1	0	0	1	1	0	3
S. Wilkins	0	0	0	0	1	0	0	0	0	0	0	0	1	0	0	1	3
E. Woodwell	0	0	0	0	0	0	0	0	0	0	1	0	0	0	0	0	1
Total	0	0	0	0	2	1	2	7	0	1	16	0	3	3	2	2	39

or while they were out of Salem and therefore not exposed to the supposedly ergotized grain (one case), or for some other reason could not have been exposed to ergot (one case—that of the 8-week-old infant referred to earlier). One of these excluded witnesses, John Londer, gave a colorful account of seeing a "thing" with a monkey's face and cock's feet. Caporael specifically cites this testimony as a probable example of ergot poisoning despite the fact that Londer stated explicitly that he had experienced the apparition 7 or 8 years before the outbreak of the Salem crisis.

The first fact uncovered by our examination was that 78 percent of the witnesses did not report suffering even a single symptom; only 18 reported suffering one or more symptoms after the ergotism is hypothesized to have begun. Most of the testimony consisted of observation made on the afflicted girls or other factual information (such as that the witness's cow died three days after the accused passed by his barn). Three witnesses testified about the death of one man and several testified about symptoms of three other individuals. Altogether, the testimony examined contained symptoms for 21 individuals other than the afflicted girls.

The first thing to note about Table 1 is that none of the witnesses reported a pattern of symptoms characteristic of convulsive ergotism. There is no evidence that any of them suffered vomiting, diarrhea, a livid skin color, permanent contractures of the extremities, a ravenous appetite, or perceptual disturbances (other than apparitions). In 10 of the 21 cases only a single symptom was reported. G. Cory reported a short-lived inability to say his prayers, and W. Putnam mimicked the gestures of one of the accused (he clenched his fist when she clenched hers and held his head in the same position as she did hers). These are obviously not cases of ergotism. In a third case, J. Putnam suffered briefly from "strange fits." The timing of these fits makes ergot an unlikely possibility. Caporael reasons that the village was exposed to ergotized rye by December 1691. Putnam reported having his fits in April 1692. It is unlikely that he would have been so late in succumbing to its effects.

In a fourth monosymptomatic case two of the afflicted girls testified that J. Holton was "tormented" by specters and that while they observed him the specters left him and began attacking them instead. Holton testified that he was immediately cured as soon as the girls reported that the specters had left him to attack them. Such an immediate alleviation of symptoms is obviously not characteristic of ergot poisoning.

In the other six monosymptomatic cases the witnesses each reported an apparition. These individuals all stated that on one or more occasions they saw a specter of some sort, usually the vivid image of an accused witch, a dead person, or an animal. All indicated belief that these imaginings were real events rather than dreams (some occurred while they were in bed) or flights of fancy. However, none of these witnesses also reported perceptual disturbances (such as halos around objects). As was pointed out above, apparition or perceptual distortions in the absence of other symptoms are not characteristic of ergot poisoning. The apparition described by these five witnesses were very similar to apparitions that five other witnesses (not included in Table 1) said they had experienced several years before the hypothesized outbreak of ergotism.

The remaining 11 witnesses in Table 1 each exhibited more than one symptom. In two of these cases (Bittford and Gould) the witnesses' experiences consisted primarily of what were probably dreams of hypnagogic experiences. Both men reported being in bed at night when they saw apparitions of accused witches. Bittford testified that his experience was accompanied by a stiffness in his neck that lasted several days, and Gould said that he was pinched twice on his side. Gould also reported a second apparition, which was followed by a pain in his foot lasting 2 or 3 days.

Daniel Wilkins died after an illness that lasted about 2 weeks. The only symptom reported about his illness was that he appeared to be choking shortly before he died, and this was reported only after the afflicted girls testified that they saw specters choking him. Wilkins did not show any sign of illness before the beginning of May 1692. For ergot to explain these events he would have had to be eating poisoned rye for 4 months without exhibiting any symptoms and then suddenly to have fallen ill and died in 2 weeks—a highly improbable occurrence.

Several symptoms are recorded for Wilkins's sister Rebecca, but she had not exhibited any of them until after a physician had diagnosed her brother's illness as preternatural and after the afflicted girls had reported seeing specters attack his body.

Another brother, S. Wilkins, reported an array of symptoms which included a pain in his hand, specters of a witch and of a black hat, falling off his horse, and a strong urge to run. None of them were experienced before June 1692.

Four persons, J. Doritch, J. Indian, T. Indian, and Mrs. Pope, displayed symptoms during the trials similar to those displayed by the afflicted girls. All convulsed and reported seeing specters that afflicted them or others. Mrs. Pope convulsed whenever an afflicted girl "saw" her about to be attacked by specters, and J. Indian's convulsions could be terminated by the touch of a witch. On one occasion Mrs. Pope also reported pain in her stomach whenever an accused witch "did but lean her Breast against the Seat." T. Indian eventually confessed that she had reported apparitions and enacted other symptoms because her master had beaten her and otherwise threatened her until she agreed to do so.

E. Keysar is the only witness in all the Salem records whose testimony includes symptoms even vaguely resembling the perceptual distortions associated with LSD. Keysar reported that, while in a darkened room, he saw "strange things" that quivered. This was immediately followed by seeing a quivering hand in his fireplace. Testimony of this type may be associated with acute anxiety and a host of other factors as well as with hallucinogenic substances. There are at least three reasons to infer that Keysar's experience was due to anxiety and expectation rather than to ergot: (i) he reported no other symptoms, (ii) the experience occurred in May 1692, five months after the time he would have begun ingesting ergot, and (iii) earlier that same day he had been severely frightened because he believed that an accused witch "did steadfastly fix [his] eyes upon me."

The final case, and the only one to exhibit as many as four of the symptoms listed in Table 1, is that of J. Bayley, who as Caporael points out did not live in Salem Village. He and his wife had spent one evening there and left the next day. On their way out of the village they passed the house of a man and wife accused of witchcraft. Bayley reported that at this point he felt a blow to his chest and a pain in his stomach. He also thought he saw the accused witches (who were jailed at the time) near the house and then became speechless for a brief period of time. Shortly thereafter he experienced another blow to the chest and thought he saw a women in the distance. When he looked again he saw a cow rather than a woman. After arriving at his home he reported feeling pinched and bitten by something invisible. His wife experienced no symptoms. Caporael says Bayley's testimony "suggests ergot." It seems far more plausible, however, that being a fervent believer in witchcraft he experienced an upsurge of anxiety as he approached the house of two convicted witches than that he ingested ergot during his stay in the village and by coincidence experienced the first symptoms of his poisoning as he happened to pass the witches' house.

Thus, the testimony of the witnesses who testified against the Salem Village witches does not support the ergot poisoning hypothesis. On the contrary, it tends to disconfirm it.

The End of the Salem Crisis

Caporael says that "the Salem witchcraft episode was an event localized in both time and space." The implication of this statement is that the episode was confined to the geographical area hypothesized to be afflicted by ergo-tized grain. However, by midsummer of 1692 individuals were being accused of witchcraft not only in Salem but also in the neighboring towns of Ames-bury, Andover, Beverly, Billerica, Boxford, Charlestown, Gloucester, Ipswich, Salisbury, and Topsfield. The Salem crisis even spurred on witch accusations in Connecticut. No one has proposed that the spreading panic resulted from a concurrent spread of ergotized rye. It is therefore worth noting that the witnesses from neighboring towns who testified against their own local witches provided the same kinds of spectral testimony that are found in the Salem records. Andover even produced its own afflicted girl.

Caporael cites a "commonly expressed observation" that the Salem witch hunt, after escalating through the summer of 1692, ended abruptly "for no apparent reason." Her own view is, apparently, that it ended abruptly be-cause the village was no longer exposed to ergotized rye. She points out that, after the crisis had passed, some of the magistrates and jurymen experienced deep remorse and had difficulty comprehending their own behavior. She suggests that ergot may have altered their thought processes during the crisis and after they regained their senses they could not understand what had happened to them.

It is important to point out that abrupt endings to large-scale panics about witchery were the rule rather than the exception. Midelfort, who has studied the many large-scale witch crises that occurred in 16th-century Germany describes the process. These crises commonly began with accusations against socially deviant and lower-class individuals. Accusations escalated quickly, and more and more prominent individuals who did not fit the popular social stereotype of a witch were accused. Inevitably, many people, including some of the prosecuting judges, became increasingly skeptical of the validity of the judicial procedures and the spectral evidence, and persons of standing took steps to bring the persecutions to an abrupt end. These crises were often followed by remorse and second thoughts on the part of some magistrates and other officials. The course of the Salem crisis was the same as that of the typical German crisis.

In summary: The available evidence does not support the hypothesis that ergot poisoning played a role in the Salem crisis. The general features of the crisis did not resemble an ergotism epidemic. The symptoms of the afflicted girls and of the other witnesses were not those of convulsive ergotism. And the abrupt ending of the crisis, and the remorse and second thoughts of those who judged and testified against the accused, can be explained without recourse to the ergotism hypothesis.

The Responsibility of
the Puritans

The word "Puritanism" has often served as a handy explanation for whatever is repressive and joyless in American life. It is not surprising then that Puritanism has been assigned much of the blame for the persecution of the witches. At the height of the Watergate scandal of the 1970s, a congressman warned that the impeachment process could turn legislators into "a set of Cotton Mathers, engaging in witch hunts, setting extraordinarily high standards for other people, though not always for themselves."

But do Cotton Mather and his fellow Puritans deserve to be singled out for blame? For if they were responsible for the witch-craze, then how can one explain the persecution of witches that took place in non-Puritan societies, such as Anglican England and Catholic France? GEORGE LYMAN KITTREDGE (1860–1941), in the early years of the twentieth century, used this line of reasoning to defend the Puritans. By examining the witch-beliefs of Europe, Kittredge tried to prove that Salem was "a very small incident in the history of a terrible superstition."

In the essay that follows, Kittredge refers to the Puritans as "our fathers." And in fact, Kittredge was a direct descendent of the first settlers of Massachusetts. To what extent did the author's desire to defend his ancestors' reputation influence his thinking?

11. A Small Chapter in an Old Superstition

The darkest page of New England history is, by common consent, that which is inscribed with the words Salem Witchcraft. The hand of the apologist trembles as it turns the leaf. The reactionary writer who prefers iconoclasm to hero-worship sharpens his pen and pours fresh gall into his inkpot when he comes to this sinister subject. Let us try to consider the matter, for a few minutes, unemotionally, and to that end let us pass in review a number of facts which may help us to look at the Witchcraft Delusion of 1692 in its due proportions—not as an abnormal outbreak of fanaticism, not as an isolated

From George Lyman Kittredge, "Notes on Witchcraft," *Proceedings of the American Antiquarian Society,* vol. XVIII (April 1907), pp. 148–212. Reprinted with the permission of the American Antiquarian Society. Footnotes omitted.

tragedy, but as a mere incident, a brief and transitory episode in the biography of a terrible, but perfectly natural, superstition.

In the first place, we know that the New Englanders did not invent the belief in witchcraft. It is a universally human belief. No race or nation is exempt from it. Formerly, it was an article in the creed of everybody in the world, and it is still held, in some form or other, and to a greater or less extent, by a large majority of mankind.

Further, our own attitude of mind toward witchcraft is a very modern attitude indeed. To us, one who asserts the existence, or even the possibility, of the crime of witchcraft staggers under a burden of proof which he cannot conceivably support. His thesis seems to us unreasonable, abnormal, monstrous; it can scarcely be stated in intelligible terms; it savors of madness. Now, before we can do any kind of justice to our forefathers—a matter, be it remembered, of no moment to them, for they have gone to their reward, but, I take it, of considerable importance to us—we must empty our heads of all such rationalistic ideas. To the contemporaries of William Stoughton and Samuel Sewall the existence of this crime was not merely an historical phenomenon, it was a fact of contemporary experience. Whoever denied the occurrence of witchcraft in the past, was an atheist; whoever refused to admit its actual possibility in the present, was either stubbornly incredulous, or destitute of the ability to draw an inference. Throughout the seventeenth century, very few persons could be found—not merely in New England, but in the whole world—who would have ventured to take so radical a position. That there had been witches and sorcerers in antiquity was beyond cavil. That there were, or might be, witches and sorcerers in the present was almost equally certain. The crime was recognized by the Bible, by all branches of the Church, by philosophy, by natural science, by the medical faculty, by the law of England. . . .

We must not leave this subject without looking into the question of numbers and dates. The history of the Salem Witchcraft is, to all intents and purposes, the sum total of witchcraft history in the whole of Massachusetts for a century. From the settlement of the country, of course, our fathers believed in witchcraft, and cases came before the courts from time to time, but, outside of the Salem outbreak, not more than half-a-dozen executions can be shown to have occurred. It is not strange that there should have been witch trials. It is inconceivable that the Colony should have passed through its first century without some special outbreak of prosecution—inconceivable, that is to say, to one who knows what went on in England and the rest of Europe during that time. The wonderful thing is not that an outbreak of prosecution occurred, but that it did not come sooner and last longer.

From the first pranks of the afflicted children in Mr. Parris's house (in February, 1692) to the collapse of the prosecution in January, 1693, was less than a year. During the interval twenty persons had suffered death, and two are known to have died in jail. If to these we add the six sporadic cases that occurred in Massachusetts before 1692, there is a total of twenty-eight; but this is the whole reckoning, not merely for a year or two but for a complete century. The concentration of the trouble in Massachusetts within the limits of a single year has given a wrong turn to the thoughts of many writers. This concentration makes the case more conspicuous, but it does not make it worse. On the contrary, it makes it better. It is astonishing that there should have been only half-a-dozen executions for witchcraft in Massachusetts before 1692, and equally astonishing that the delusion, when it became acute, should have raged for but a year, and that but twenty-two persons should have lost their lives. The facts are distinctly creditable to our ancestors—to their moderation and to the rapidity with which their good sense could reassert itself after a brief eclipse.

Let us compare figures a little. For Massachusetts the account is simple—twenty-eight victims in a century. No one has ever made an accurate count of the executions in England during the seventeenth century, but they must have mounted into the hundreds. Matthew Hopkins, the Witch-finder General, brought at least two hundred to the gallows from 1645 to 1647. In Scotland the number of victims was much larger. The most conscientiously moderate estimate makes out a total of at least 3,400 between the years 1580 and 1680, and the computer declares that future discoveries in the way of records may force us to increase this figure very much. On the Continent many thousands suffered death in the sixteenth and seventeenth centuries. Mannhardt reckons the victims from the fourteenth to the seventeenth century at millions, and half a million is thought to be a moderate estimate. In Alsace, a hundred and thirty-four witches and wizards were burned in 1582 on one occasion, the execution taking place on the 15th, 19th, 24th, and 28th of October. Nicholas Remy (Remigius) of Lorraine gathered the materials for his work on the Worship of Demons, published in 1595, from the trials of some 900 persons whom he had sentenced to death in the fifteen years preceding. In 1609, de Lancre and his associate are said to have condemned 700 in the Basque country in four months. The efforts of the Bishop of Bamberg from 1622 to 1633 resulted in six hundred executions; the Bishop of Wurzburg, in about the same period, put nine hundred persons to death. These figures, which might be multiplied almost indefinitely, help us to look at the Salem Witchcraft in its true proportions—as a very small incident in the history of a terrible superstition.

These figures may perhaps be attacked as involving a fallacious comparison, inasmuch as we have not attempted to make the relative population of New England and the several districts referred to a factor in the equation. Such an objection, if anybody should see fit to make it, is easily answered by other figures. The total number of victims in Massachusetts from the first settlement to the end of the seventeenth century was, as we have seen, twenty-eight—or thirty-four for the whole of New England. Compare the following figures, taken from the annals of Great Britain and Scotland alone. In 1612, ten witches were executed belonging to a single district of Lancashire. In 1645 twenty-nine witches were condemned at once in a single Hundred in Essex, eighteen were hanged at once at Bury in Suffolk—"and a hundred and twenty more were to have been tried, but a sudden movement of the king's troops in that direction obliged the judges to adjourn the session." Under date of July 26, 1645, Whitelocke records that "20 Witches in Norfolk were executed," and again, under April 15, 1650, that "at a little Village within two miles [of Berwick] two Men and three Women were burnt for Witches, and nine more were to be burnt, the Village consisting of but fourteen Families, and there were as many witches" and further that "twenty more were to be burnt within six Miles of that place." If we pass over to the Continent, the numbers are appalling. Whether, then, we take the in computation in gross or in detail, New England emerges from the test with credit. . . .

Why did the Salem outbreak occur? Of course there were many causes—some of which have already suggested themselves in the course of our discussion. But one fact should be borne in mind as of particular importance. The belief in witchcraft, as we have already had occasion to remark, was a constant quantity; but outbreaks of prosecution came, in England—and, generally speaking, elsewhere—spasmodically, at irregular intervals. If we look at Great Britain for a moment, we shall see that such outbreaks are likely to coincide with times of political excitement or anxiety. Thus early in Elizabeth's reign, when everything was more or less unsettled, Bishop Jewel, whom all historians delight to honor, made a deliberate and avowed digression, in a sermon before the queen, in order to warn her that witchcraft was rampant in the realm, to inform her (on the evidence of his own eyes) that her subjects were being injured in their goods and their health, and to exhort her to enforce the law. The initial zeal of James I in the prosecution of witches stood in close connection with the trouble he was having with his turbulent cousin Francis Bothwell. The operations of Matthew Hopkins (in 1645–1647) were a mere accompaniment to the tumult of the Civil War; the year in which they began was the year of Laud's execution and of the Battle of Naseby. The Restoration was followed by a fresh outbreak of witch prosecution—mild in England, though far-reaching in its consequences, but very sharp in Scotland.

With facts like these in view, we can hardly regard it as an accident that the Salem witchcraft marks a time when the Colony was just emerging from a political struggle that had threatened its very existence. For several years men's minds had been on the rack. The nervous condition of public feeling is wonderfully well depicted in a letter written in 1688 by the Rev. Joshua Moodey in Boston to Increase Mather, then in London as agent of the Colony. The Colonists are much pleased by the favor with which Mather has been received, but they distrust court promises. They are alarmed by a report that Mather and his associates have suffered "a great slurr" on account of certain overzealous actions. Moodey rejoices in the death of Robert Mason, "one of the worst enemies that you & I & Mr. Morton had in these parts." Then there are the Indians: "The cloud looks very dark and black upon us, & wee are under very awfull circumstances, which render an Indian Warr terrible to us." The Colonists shudder at a rumor that John Palmer, one of Andros's Council, is to come over as Supreme Judge, and know not how to reconcile it with the news of the progress their affairs have been making with the King. And finally, the writer gives an account of the case of Goodwin's afflicted children, which, as we know, was a kind of prologue to the Salem outbreak: "Wee have a very strange th[ing] among us, which we know not what to make of, except it bee Witchcraft, as we think it must needs bee." Clearly, there would have been small fear, in 1692, of a plot on Satan's part to destroy the Province, if our forefathers had not recently encountered other dangers of a more tangible kind.

In conclusion, I may venture to sum up, in the form of a number of brief theses, the main results at which we appear to have arrived in our discussion of witchcraft:

1. The belief in witchcraft is the common heritage of humanity. It is not chargeable to any particular time, or race, or form of religion.

2. Witchcraft in some shape or other is still credited by a majority of the human race.

3. The belief in witchcraft was practically universal in the seventeenth century, even among the educated; with the mass of the people it was absolutely universal.

4. To believe in witchcraft in the seventeenth century was no more

discreditable to a man's head or heart than it was to believe in spontaneous generation or to be ignorant of the germ theory of disease.

5. The position of the seventeenth-century believers in witchcraft was logically and theologically stronger than that of the few persons who rejected the current belief.

6. The impulse to put a witch to death comes from the instinct of self-preservation. It is no more cruel or otherwise blameworthy, in itself, than the impulse to put a murderer to death.

7. The belief in witchcraft manifests itself, not in steady and continuous prosecution, but in sudden outbreaks occurring at irregular intervals.

8. Such outbreaks are not symptoms of extraordinary superstition or of a peculiarly acute state of unreason. They are due, like other panics, to a perturbed condition of the public mind. Hence they are likely to accompany, or to follow, crises in politics or religion.

9. The responsibility for any witch prosecution rests primarily on the community or neighborhood as a whole, not on the judge or the jury.

10. No jury, whether in a witch trial or in any other case, can be more enlightened than the general run of the vicinage.

11. Many persons who have been executed for witchcraft have supposed themselves to be guilty and have actually been guilty in intent.

12. Practically every person executed for witchcraft believed in the reality of such a crime, whether he supposed himself to be guilty of it or not.

13. The witch beliefs of New England were brought over from the Mother Country by the first settlers.

14. Spectral evidence had been admitted in the examinations and trials of witches in England for a hundred years before the Salem prosecutions took place.

15. Trials, convictions, and executions for witchcraft occurred in England after they had come to an end in Massachusetts, and they occurred on the Continent a hundred years later than that time.

16. Spectral evidence was admitted in English witch trials after such trials had ceased in Massachusetts.

17. The total number of persons executed for witchcraft in New England from the first settlement to the end of the century is inconsiderable, especially in view of what was going on in Europe.

18. The public repentance and recantation of judge and jury in Massachusetts have no parallel in the history of witchcraft.

19. The repentance and recantation came at a time which made them singularly effective arguments in the hands of the opponents of the witch dogma in England.

20. The record of New England in the matter of witchcraft is highly credit-able, when considered as a whole and from the comparative point of view.

21. It is easy to be wise after the fact, especially when the fact is two hundred years old.

The following essay was written by PERRY MILLER (1905–1963), a professor of American literature at Harvard and a highly regarded student of Puritan thought. Here Miller was not as concerned with the guilt or innocence of the seventeenth centu-ry Puritans as he was with the effects of the witchcraft outbreak on the intellectual his-tory of New England. According to Miller, the events at Salem shook the Puritans' confidence in a fundamental aspect of their faith: their "federal covenant" with God. The people of Massachusetts believed that their society was bound in a special relationship with God—a covenant—which obligated them to observe His will. In 1692 the Puritans believed that they were observing that divine will when they hunted down the witches in their midst. But something went wrong: their desire to obey God resulted in tragedy. Miller shows how this crisis affected three leading Puritans: Cotton Mather, the author of The Wonders of the Invisible World; *John Hale, a clergyman who had also defended the execution of the witches; and Samuel Sewall, one of the Salem judges.*

12. The Puritans and the Witches

To comprehend the predicament of the Puritan intellect in 1692, we should note that earlier in the crisis Cotton Mather preached one of his most stirring jeremiads, *A Midnight Cry,* in which he trounced New England with the gory threat of Indian atrocities: they "have taken our Brethren, and binding them to a Stake, with a Lingering Heat, Burned and Roasted them to Death; the Exquisite Groans and Shrieks of those our Dying Bretheren should Awaken us." In the intoxication of such external dangers, he publicly committed himself to the thesis that internal traitors had been convicted "by so fair and full a process of Law, as would render the Denyers thereof worthy of no Reasonabler Company than that in Bedlam." But his *Diary* shows him wres-tling with the doubt that corrodes the pages of the *Wonders*; by June 7, 1694, he had openly to declare that the affliction consisted not so much in a descent of evil angels as in "unheard of DELUSIONS." At the election of May 27, 1696, he was simply nonplussed: "It was, and it will be, past all Humane Skill,

From Perry Miller, *The New England Mind: From Colony to Province* (Cambridge, Mass.: Harvard University Press, 1953). Reprinted by permission of the Harvard University Press. Copyright © 1953 by the President and Fellows of Harvard College.

Exactly to Understand what Inextricable Things we have met withal." In 1697 he had the honesty in his life of Phips (and later the integrity to incorporate the passage into the *Magnalia*) to acknowledge that the court had operated upon an erroneous notion; he still, though lamely, insisted that there had been other proofs, but in a last agony could not prevent himself from recording: "Nevertheless, divers were condemned, against whom the chief evidence was founded in the spectral exhibitions."

In the privacy of his *Diary*, Cotton Mather could simultaneously tell himself, even in 1692, that he always testified against spectral evidence and that the judges were "a most charming Instance of Prudence and Patience." Because he spoke "honourably" of their persons (at least according to his own account), "the mad people thro' the Countrey . . . reviled mee, as if I had been the Doer of all the hard Things, that were done, in the Prosecution of the Witchcraft." Considering that there is ample evidence in the *Diary* (all the more remarkable because it is studiously composed) that he never succeeded in persuading himself he had done the right thing (in 1697, after Sewall had repented, he grew panicky lest the Lord take revenge upon his family "for my not appearing with Vigor enough to stop the proceedings of the Judges"), it is the more striking that there are no respects in which one can say that the clergy suffered any immediate diminution of prestige or influence because of witchcraft. Nor did the judges lose standing in the community: neither Stoughton, who never admitted error, nor Samuel Sewall, who, in one of the noblest gestures of the period, took the shame of it upon himself before his church. The real effect of the tragedy is not to be traced in the field of politics or society, but in the intangible area of federal theory, and in the still more intangible region of self-esteem.

Henceforth there was, although for a time desperately concealed, a flaw in the very foundation of the covenant conception. The doctrine that afflictions are punishments to be dispelled by confession had produced at least one ghastly blunder; repentance had been twisted into a ruse, and the civil magistrate, by a vigorous exercise of his appointed function, had become guilty of hideous enormities. Nineteen years later, Cotton Mather was still keeping vigils to inquire of the Lord "the meaning of the Descent from the Invisible World," and was obliged repeatedly to discharge his sense of guilt by advertising, as a fundamental tenet of New England along with liberty of conscience, "That Persons are not to be judg'd Confederates with Evil Spirits, meerly because the Evil Spirits do make possessed People cry out upon them." The meaning of New England had been fixed, by Winthrop and the founders, in the language of a covenant; if henceforth there was so much as a shadow of suspicion upon that philosophy, in what realm of significance could the land hold its identity?

John Hale, we have seen, was one of three ministers who committed themselves; in his revulsion, he went so far to the other extreme that Sewall feared he would deny witchcraft itself. He wrote *A Modest Enquiry Into the Nature of Witchcraft* in 1698; it is a sad, troubled, and honest book, which he could not bring himself to publish, so that it appeared two years after his death, in 1702. It passed unnoted, and is of importance mainly for the light it sheds upon the working of many minds obliged to live with perplexity. For the fact could not be got round: Hale had been trained to a belief in certain articles, and precisely these fundamentals "I here question as unsafe to be used." Nobody in New England had yet uttered such a sentence. Once the process of "a more strict scanning of the principles I had imbibed" was started, once it led to a rejection of any of the principles of aged, learned, and judicious persons, where would it stop? We followed (with a "kind of Implicit Faith") the "traditions of our fathers," and now see that they, "weighed in the balance of the Sanctuary, are found too light." The whole edifice of the New England mind rocked at the very thought that it might be based, not upon a cosmic design of the covenant, but merely upon fallible founders; yet Hale forced himself to recognize the power of conditioning: "A Child will not easily forsake the principles he hath been trained up in from his Cradle."

Frightened by his own audacity, Hale turned back at the end of his soliloquy: because our fathers did not see deeply into these mysteries, let us not undervalue the good foundations they did lay. They brought the land into an engagement with God, and He may even yet not entirely "cut off the Entail of his Covenant Mercies." In 1720, Samuel Sewall had his memories come thick upon him as he read the account in Neal's *History*, and cried out, "The good and gracious God be pleased to save New England and me, and my family!" The onus of error lay heavy upon the land; realization of it slowly but irresistibly ate into the New England conscience. For a long time dismay did not translate itself into a disbelief in witchcraft or into anticlericalism, but it rapidly became an unassuageable grief that the covenanted community should have committed an irreparable evil. Out of sorrow and chagrin, out of dread, was born a new love for the land which had been desecrated, but somehow also consecrated, by the blood of innocents.

New Directions

With a few exceptions, the historians represented in this book were preoccupied with the search for an explanation of the incidents of alleged witchcraft at Salem. For example, Charles Upham blamed the afflicted girls, Ernest Caulfield blamed Puritan society, Chadwick Hansen blamed (in part) the witches. The following essay by JOHN DEMOS (b. 1937), a professor of American history at Brandeis University, is notable for its explicit rejection of a line of inquiry that seeks to assign culpability. The questions raised here concern the social and psychological characteristics of the principal actors. Demos studies New England witchcraft not as an end in itself, but as a way of opening what he describes as a "window on the irrational"—a window that most historians have avoided.

13. Underlying Themes

It is faintly embarrassing for a historian to summon his colleagues to still another consideration of early New England witchcraft. Here, surely, is a topic that previous generations of writers have sufficiently worked, indeed overworked. Samuel Eliot Morison once commented that the Salem witch-hunt was, after all, "but a small incident in the history of a great superstition"; and Perry Miller noted that with only minor qualifications "the intellectual history of New England can be written as though no such thing ever happened. It had no effect on the ecclesiastical or political situation, it does not figure in the institutional or ideological development." Popular interest in the subject is, then, badly out of proportion to its actual historical significance, and perhaps the sane course for the future would be silence.

This assessment seems, on the face of it, eminently sound. Witchcraft was not an important matter from the standpoint of the larger historical process; it exerted only limited influence on the unfolding sequence of events in colonial New England. Moreover, the literature on the subject seems to have reached a point of diminishing returns. Details of fact have been endlessly canvassed, and the main outlines of the story, particularly the story of Salem, are well and widely known.

From John Demos, "Underlying Themes in the Witchcraft of Seventeenth-Century New England," *American Historical Review*, LXXV (June 1970), pp. 1311–1326. Reprinted by permission of the author. Footnotes omitted.

There is, to be sure, continuing debate over one set of issues: the roles played by the persons most directly involved. Indeed the historiography of Salem can be viewed, in large measure, as an unending effort to judge the participants—and, above all, to affix blame. A number of verdicts have been fashionable at one time or another. Thus the ministers were really at fault; or Cotton Mather in particular; or the whole culture of Puritanism; or the core group of "afflicted girls" (if their "fits" are construed as conscious fraud). The most recent, and in some ways most sophisticated, study of the Salem trials plunges right into the middle of the same controversy; the result is yet another conclusion. Not the girls, not the clergy, not Puritanism, but the accused witches themselves are now the chief culprits. For "witchcraft actually did exist and was widely practiced in seventeenth-century New England"; and women like Goody Glover, Bridget Bishop, and Mammy Redd were "in all probability" guilty as charged.

Clearly these questions of personal credit and blame can still generate lively interest, but are they the most fruitful, the most important questions to raise about witchcraft? Will such a debate ever be finally settled? Are its partisan terms and moral tone appropriate to historical scholarship?

The situation is not hopeless if only we are willing to look beyond the limits of our own discipline. There is, in particular, a substantial body of interesting and relevant work by anthropologists. Many recent studies of primitive societies contain chapters about witchcraft, and there are several entire monographs on the subject. The approach they follow differs strikingly from anything in the historical literature. Broadly speaking, the anthropological work is far more analytic, striving always to use materials on witchcraft as a set of clues or "symptoms." The subject is important not in its own right but as a means of exploring certain larger questions about the society. For example, witchcraft throws light on social structure, on the organization of families, and on the inner dynamics of personality. The substance of such investigation, of course, varies greatly from one culture to another, but the framework, the informing purposes are roughly the same. To apply this framework and these purposes to historical materials is not inherently difficult. The data may be inadequate in a given case, but the analytic categories themselves are designed for any society, whether simple or complex, Western or non-Western, past or contemporary. Consider, by way of illustration, the strategy proposed for the main body of this essay.

Our discussion will focus on a set of complex relationships between the alleged witches and their victims. The former group will include all persons accused of practicing witchcraft, and they will be called, simply, witches. The category of victims will comprise everyone who claimed to have suffered from witchcraft, and they will be divided into two categories to account for an important distinction between different kinds of victims. As every school-child knows, some victims experienced fits—bizarre seizures that, in the language of modern psychiatry, closely approximate the clinical picture of hysteria. These people may be called accusers, since their sufferings and their accusations seem to have carried the greatest weight in generating formal proceedings against witches. A second, much larger group of victims includes people who attributed to witchcraft some particular misfortune they had suffered, most typically an injury or illness, the sudden death of domestic animals, the loss of personal property, or repeated failure in important day-to-day activities like farming, fishing, and hunting. This type of evidence was of secondary importance in trials of witches and was usually brought forward after the accusers had pressed their own more damaging charges. For people testifying to such experiences, therefore, the shorthand term witnesses seems reasonably appropriate.

Who were these witches, accusers, and witnessses? How did their lives intersect? Most important, what traits were generally characteristic and what traits were alleged to have been characteristic of each group? These will be the organizing questions in the pages that follow. Answers to these questions will treat both external (or objective) circumstances and internal (or subjective) experiences. In the case of witches, for example, it is important to try to discover their age, marital status, socioeconomic position, and visible personality traits. But it is equally important to examine the characteristics attributed to witches by others—flying about at night, transforming themselves into animals, and the like. In short, one can construct a picture of witches in fact and in fantasy; and comparable efforts can be made with accusers and witnesses. Analysis directed to the level of external reality helps to locate certain points of tension or conflict in the social structure of a community. The fantasy picture, on the other hand, reveals more directly the psychological dimension of life, the inner preoccupations, anxieties, and conflicts of individual members of that community.

Such an outline looks deceptively simple, but in fact it demands an unusual degree of caution, from writer and reader alike. The approach is explicitly cross-disciplinary, reaching out to anthropology for strategy and to psychology for theory. There is, of course, nothing new about the idea of a working relationship between history and the behavioral sciences. It is more than ten years since William Langer's famous summons to his colleagues to consider this their "next assignment"; but the record of actual output is still very meager. All such efforts remain quite experimental; they are designed more to stimulate discussion than to prove a definitive case.

There is a final point—about context and the larger purposes of this form of inquiry. Historians have traditionally worked with purposeful, conscious events, "restricting themselves," in Langer's words "to recorded fact and to strictly rational motivation." They have not necessarily wished to exclude non-rational or irrational behavior, but for the most part they have done so. Surely in our own post-Freudian era there is both need and opportunity to develop a more balanced picture. It is to these long-range ends that further study of witchcraft should be dedicated. For witchcraft is, if nothing else, an open window on the irrational.

The first witchcraft trial of which any record survives occurred at Windsor, Connecticut, in 1647, and during the remainder of the century the total of cases came to nearly one hundred. Thirty-eight people were executed as witches, and a few more, though convicted, managed somehow to escape the death penalty. There were, of course, other outcomes as well: full-dress trials resulting in acquittal, hung juries, convictions reversed on appeal, and "complaints" filed but not followed up. Finally, no doubt, many unrecorded episodes touching on witchcraft, episodes of private suspicion or public gossip, never eventuated in legal action at all.

This long series of witchcraft cases needs emphasis lest the Salem outbreak completely dominate our field of vision. Salem differed radically from previous episodes in sheer scope; it developed a degree of self-reinforcing momentum present in no other instance. But it was very similar in many qualitative aspects: the types of people concerned, the nature of the charges, the fits, and so forth. Indeed, from an analytic standpoint, all these cases can be regarded as roughly equivalent and interchangeable. They are pieces of a single, larger phenomenon, a system of witchcraft belief that was generally prevalent in early New England. The evidence for such a system must, of course, be drawn from a variety of cases to produce representative conclusions. For most questions this is quite feasible; there is more evidence, from a greater range of cases, than can ever be presented in a single study.

Yet in one particular matter the advantages of concentrating on Salem are overwhelming. It affords a unique opportunity to portray the demography of witchcraft, to establish a kind of profile for each of the three basic categories of people involved in witchcraft, in terms of sex, age, and marital status. Thus the statistical tables that follow are drawn entirely from detailed work on the Salem materials. The earlier cases do not yield the breadth of data necessary for this type of quantitative investigation. They do, however, provide many fragments of evidence that are generally consistent with the Salem picture.

There is at least minimal information about 165 people accused as witches during the entire period of the Salem outbreak.

Sex	Total	Marital Status	Male	Female	Total	Age	Male	Female	Total
Male	42	Single	8	29	37	Under 20	6	18	24
Female	120	Married	15	61	76	21–30	3	7	10
		Widowed	1	20	21	31–40	3	8	11
Total	162					41–50	6	18	24
		Total	24	110	134	51–60	5	23	28
						61–70	4	8	12
						Over 70	3	6	9
						Total	30	88	118

These figures point to an important general conclusion: the witches were predominantly married or widowed women, between the ages of forty-one and sixty. While the exceptions add up to a considerable number, most of them belonged to the families of middle-aged, female witches. Virtually all the young persons in the group can be identified as children of witches and most of the men as husbands of witches. In fact this pattern conformed to an assumption then widely prevalent, that the transmission of witchcraft would naturally follow the lines of family or of close friendship. An official statement from the government of Connecticut included among the "grounds for Examination of a Witch" the following:

> if ye party suspected by ye son or daughter the servt or familiar friend; neer Neighbor or old Companion of a Knowne or Convicted witch this alsoe a presumton for witchcraft is an art yt may be learned & Convayd from man to man & oft it falleth out yt a witch dying leaveth som of ye aforesd. heirs of her witchcraft.

In short, young witches and male witches belonged to a kind of derivative category. They were not the prime targets in these situations; they were, in a literal sense, rendered suspect by association. The deepest suspicions, the most intense anxieties, remained fixed on middle-aged women.

Thirty-four persons experienced fits of one sort or another during the Salem trials and qualify thereby as accusers.

Sex	Total	Marital Status	Male	Female	Total	Age	Male	Female	Total
Male	5	Single	5	23	28	Under 11	0	1	1
Female	29	Married	0	6	6	11–15	1	7	8
		Widowed	0	0	0	16–20	1	13	14
Total	34					21–25	0	1	1
		Total	5	29	34	26–30	0	1	1
						Over 30	0	4	4
						Total	2	27	29

Here again the sample shows a powerful cluster. The vast majority of the accusers were single girls between the ages of eleven and twenty. The exceptions in this case (two boys, three males of undetermined age, and four adult women) are rather difficult to explain, for there is little evidence about any of them. By and large, however, they played only a minor role in the trials. Perhaps the matter can be left this way: the core group of accusers was entirely composed of adolescent girls, but the inner conflicts so manifest in their fits found an echo in at least a few persons of other ages or of other ages or of the opposite sex.

Eighty-four persons came forward as witnesses at one time or another during the Salem trials.

Sex	Total	Marital Status	Male	Female	Total	Age	Male	Female	Total
Male	63	Single	11	3	14	Under 20	3	2	5
Female	21	Married	39	16	55	21–30	13	4	17
		Widowed	3	1	4	31–40	14	6	20
Total	84					41–50	18	7	25
		Total	53	20	73	51–60	11	1	12
						61–70	2	1	3
						Over 70	2	0	2
						Total	63	21	84

Here the results seem relatively inconclusive. Three-fourths of the witnesses were men, but a close examination of the trial records suggests a simple reason for this: men were more likely, in seventeenth-century England, to take an active part in legal proceedings of any type. When a husband and wife were victimized together by some sort of witchcraft, it was the former who would normally come forward to testify. As to the ages of the witnesses, there is a fairly broad distribution between twenty and sixty years. Probably, then, this category reflects the generalized belief in witchcraft among all elements of the community in a way that makes it qualitatively different from the groupings of witches and accusers.

There is much more to ask about external realities in the lives of such people, particularly with regard to their social and economic position. Unfortunately, however, the evidence is somewhat limited here and permits only a few impressionistic observations. It seems that many witches came from the lower levels of the social structure, but there were too many exceptions to see in this a really significant pattern. The first three accused at Salem were Tituba, a Negro slave, Sarah Good, the wife of a poor laborer, and Sarah Osbourne, who possessed a very considerable estate. Elizabeth Godman, tried at New Haven in 1653, seems to have been poor and perhaps a beggar; but Nathaniel and Rebecca Greensmith, who were convicted and executed at Hartford eight years later, were quite well-to-do; and "Mistress" Ann Hibbens, executed at Boston in 1656, was the widow of a wealthy merchant and former magistrate of the Bay Colony.

What appears to have been common to nearly all these people, irrespective of their economic position, was some kind of personal eccentricity, some deviant or even criminal behavior that had long since marked them out as suspect. Some of them had previously been tried for theft or battery or slander; others were known for their interest in dubious activites like fortune-telling or certain kinds of folk-healing. The "witch Glover" of Boston, on whom Cotton Mather reports at some length, was Irish and Catholic, and spoke Gaelic; and a Dutch family in Hartford came under suspicion at the time the Greensmiths were tried.

More generally, many of the accused seem to have been unusually irascible and contentious in their personal relations. Years before her conviction for witchcraft Mrs. Hibbens had obtained a reputation for "natural crabbedness of . . . temper"; indeed she had been excommunicated by the Boston church in 1640, following a long and acrimonious ecclesiastical trial. William Hubbard, whose *General History of New England* was published in 1680, cited her case to make the general point that "persons of hard favor and turbulent passions are apt to be condemned by the common people as witches, upon very slight grounds." In the trial of Mercy Desborough, at Fairfield, Connecticut, in 1692, the court received numerous reports of her quarrelsome behavior. She had, for example, told one neighbor "yt shee would make him bare as a bird's tale," and to another she had repeatedly said "many hard words." Goodwife Clawson, tried at the same time, was confronted with testimony like the following:

Abigail Wescot saith that as shee was going along the street goody Clasen came out to her and they had some words together and goody Clason took up stones and threw at her: and at another time as shee went along the street before sd Clasons dore goody Clason caled to mee and asked mee what was in my Chamber last Sabbath day night; and I doe afirme that I was not there that night: and at another time as I was in her sone Steephens house being neere her one hous shee folowed me in and contended with me becase I did not com into her hous caling of me proud slut what—are you proud of your fine cloths and you love to be mistres but you neuer shal be and several other provoking speeches.

The case of Mary and Hugh Parsons, tried at Springfield in 1651, affords a further look at the external aspects of our subject. A tax rating taken at Springfield in 1646 records the landholdings of most of the principals in the witchcraft prosecutions of five years later. When the list is arranged according to wealth, Parsons falls near the middle (twenty-fourth out of forty-two), and those who testified against him come from the top, middle, and bottom. This outcome tends to confirm the general point that economic position is not, for present purposes, a significant datum. What seems, on the basis of the actual testimonies at the trial, to have been much more important was the whole dimension of eccentric and anti-social behavior. Mary Parsons, who succumbed repeatedly to periods of massive depression, was very nearly insane. During the witchcraft investigations she began by testifying against her husband and ended by convicting herself of the murder of their infant child. Hugh Parsons was a sawyer and brickmaker by trade, and there are indications that in performing these services he was sometimes suspected of charging extortionate rates. But what may have weighed most heavily against him was his propensity for prolonged and bitter quarreling; many examples of his "threatening speeches" were reported in court.

One other aspect of this particular episode is worth noting, namely, the apparent influence of spatial proximity. When the names of Parsons and his "victims" are checked against a map of Springfield in this period, it becomes very clear that the latter were mostly his nearest neighbors. In fact nearly all of the people who took direct part in the trial came from the southern half of the town. No other witchcraft episode yields such a detailed picture in this respect, but many separate pieces of evidence suggest that neighborhood antagonism was usually an aggravating factor.

We can summarize the major characteristics of the external side of New England witchcraft as follows: First, the witches themselves were chiefly women of middle age whose accusers were girls about one full generation younger. This may reflect the kind of situation that anthropologists would call a structural conflict—that is, some focus of tension created by the specific ways in which a community arranges the lives of its members. In a broad sense it is quite probable that adolescent girls in early New England were particularly subject to the control of older women, and this may well have given rise to a powerful underlying resentment. By contrast, the situation must have been less difficult for boys, since their work often took them out of the household and their behavior generally was less restricted.

There are, moreover, direct intimations of generational conflict in the witchcraft records themselves. Consider a little speech by one of the afflicted girls during a fit, a speech meticulously recorded by Cotton Mather. The words are addressed to the "specter" of a witch, with whom the girl has been having a heated argument:

> What's that? Must the younger Women, do yee say, hearken to the El-der?—They must be another Sort of Elder Women than You then! they must not bee Elder Witches, I am sure. Pray, do you for once Hearken to mee.—What a dreadful Sight are You! An Old Woman, an Old Servant of the Divel!

Second, it is notable that most witches were deviant persons—eccentric or conspicuously anti-social or both. This suggests very clearly the impact of belief in witchcraft as a form of control in the social ordering of New England communities. Here indeed is one of the most widely-founded social functions of witchcraft; its importance has been documented for many societies all over the world. Any individual who contemplates actions of which the commu-nity disapproves knows that if he performs such acts, he will become more vulnerable either to a direct attack by witches or to the charge that he is himself a witch. Such knowledge is a powerful inducement to self-constraint.

What can be said of the third basic conclusion, that witchcraft charges particularly involved neighbors? Very briefly, it must be fitted with other aspects of the social setting in these early New England communities. That there was a great deal of contentiousness among these people is suggested by innumerable court cases from the period dealing with disputes about land, lost cattle, trespass, debt, and so forth. Most men seem to have felt that the New World offered them a unique opportunity to increase their properties, and this may have heightened competitive feelings and pressures. On the other hand, cooperation was still the norm in many areas of life, not only in local govern-ment but for a variety of agricultural tasks as well. In such ambivalent circumstances it is hardly surprising that relations between close neighbors were often tense or downright abrasive.

"In all the Witchcraft which now Grievously Vexes us, I know not whether any thing be more Unaccountable, than the Trick which the Witches have, to render themselves and their Tools Invisible." Thus wrote Cotton Mather in 1692; and three centuries later it is still the "invisible" part of witchcraft that holds a special fascination. Time has greaty altered the language for such phenomena—"shapes" and "specters" have become "hallucinations"; "enchantments" are a form of "suggestion"; the Devil himself seems a fantasy—and there is a corresponding change of meanings. Yet here was something truly remarkable, a kind of irreducible core of the entire range of witchcraft phenomena. How much of it remains "unaccountable"? To ask the question is to face directly the other side of our subject: witchcraft viewed as psychic process, as a function of internal reality.

The biggest obstacles to the study of psycho-history ordinarily are practical ones involving severe limitations of historical data. Yet for witchcraft the situation is uniquely promising on these very grounds. Even a casual look at writings like Cotton Mather's *Memorable Providences* or Samuel Willard's *A briefe account* etc. discloses material so rich in psychological detail as to be nearly the equivalent of clinical case reports. The court records on witchcraft are also remarkably full in this respect. The clergy, the judges, all the leaders whose positions carried special responsibility for combatting witchcraft, regarded publicity as a most important weapon. Witchcraft would yield to careful study and the written exchange of information. Both Mather and Willard received "afflicted girls" into their own homes and recorded "possession" behavior over long periods of time.

A wealth of evidence does not, of course, by itself win the case for a psychological approach to witchcraft. Further problems remain, problems of language and of validation. There is, moreover, the very basic problem of selecting from among a variety of different theoretical models. Psychology is not a monolith, and every psycho-historian must declare a preference. In opting for psycho-analytic theory, for example, he performs, in part, an act of faith, faith that this theory provides deeper, fuller insights into human behavior than any other. In the long run the merit of such choices will probably be measured on pragmatic grounds. Does the interpretation explain materials that would otherwise remain unused? Is it consistent with evidence in related subject areas?

If, then, the proof lies in the doing, let us turn back to the New England witches and especially to their "Trick . . . to render themselves and their tools Invisible." What characterized these spectral witches? What qualities were attributed to them by the culture at large.

The most striking observation about witches is that they gave free rein to a whole gamut of hostile and aggressive feelings. In fact most witchcraft episodes began after some sort of actual quarrel. The fits of Mercy Short followed an abusive encounter with the convicted witch Sarah Good. The witch Glover was thought to have attacked Martha Goodwin after an argument about some missing clothes. Many such examples could be accumulated here, but the central message seems immediately obvious: never antagonize witches, for they will invariably strike back hard. Their compulsion to attack was, of course, most dramatically visible in the fits experienced by some of their victims. These fits were treated as tortures imposed directly and in every detail by witches or by the Devil himself. It is also significant that witches often assumed the shape of animals in order to carry out their attacks.

Animals, presumably, are not subject to constraints of either an internal or external kind; their aggressive impulses are immediately translated into action.

Another important facet of the lives of witches was their activity in company with each other. In part this consisted of long and earnest conferences on plans to overthrow the kingdom of God and replace it with the reign of the Devil. Often, however, these meetings merged with feasts, the witches' main form of self-indulgence. Details are a bit thin here, but we know that the usual beverage was beer or wine (occasionally described as bearing a suspicious resemblance to blood), and the food was bread or meat. It is also worth noting what did not happen on these occasions. There were a few reports of dancing and "sport," but very little of the wild excitements associated with witch revels in continental Europe. Most striking of all is the absence of allusions to sex; there is no nakedness, no promiscuity, no obscene contact with the Devil. This seems to provide strong support for the general proposition that the psychological conflicts underlying the early New England belief in witchcraft had much more to do with aggressive impulses than with libidinal ones.

The persons who acted as accusers also merit the closest possible attention, for the descriptions of what they suffered in their fits are perhaps the most revealing of all source materials for present purposes. They experienced, in the first place, severe pressures to go over to the Devil's side themselves. Witches approached them again and again, mixing threats and bribes in an effort to break down their Christian loyalties. Elizabeth Knapp, bewitched at Groton, Massachusetts, in 1671, was alternately tortured and plied with offers of "money, silkes, fine cloaths, ease from labor"; in 1692 Ann Foster of Andover confessed to being won over by a general promise of "prosperity," and in the same year Andrew Carrier accepted the lure of "a house and land in Andover." The same pattern appears most vividly in Cotton Mather's record of another of Mercy Short's confrontations with a spectral witch:

> "Fine promises!" she says, "You'l bestow an Husband upon mee, if I'l be your Servant. An Husband! What? A Divel! I shall then bee finely fitted with an Husband: . . . Fine Clothes! Such as Your Friend Sarah Good had, who hardly had Rags to cover her! . . . Never Dy! What? Is my Life in Your Hands? No, if it had, You had killed mee long before this Time!— What's that?—So you can!—Do it then, if You can. Come, I dare you: Here, I challenge You to do it. Kill mee if you can. . . .

Some of these promises attributed to the Devil touch the most basic human concerns (like death) and others reflect the special preoccupations (with future husbands, for example) of adolescent girls. All of them imply a kind of covetousness generally consistent with the pattern of neighborhood conflict and tension mentioned earlier.

But the fits express other themes more powerfully still, the vital problem of aggression being of central importance. The seizures themselves have the essential character of attacks: in one sense, physical attacks by the witches on the persons of the accusers and in another sense, verbal attacks by the accusers on the reputations and indeed the very lives of the witches. This points directly toward one of the most important inner processes involved in witchcraft, the process psychologists call "projection," defined roughly as "escape from repressed conflict by attributing . . . emotional drives to the external world." In short, the dynamic core of belief in witchcraft in early New England was the difficulty experienced by many individuals in finding ways to handle their own aggressive impulses. Witchcraft accusation provided one of the few approved outlets for such impulses in Puritan culture. Aggression was thus denied in the self and attributed directly to others. The accuser says, in effect: "I am not attacking you; you are attacking me!" In reality, however, the accuser is attacking the witch, and in an extremely dangerous manner, too. Witchcraft enables him to have it both ways; the impulse is denied and gratified at the same time.

The seizures of the afflicted children also permitted them to engage in a considerable amount of direct aggression. They were not, of course, held personally responsible; it was always the fault of the Devil at work inside them. Sometimes these impulses were aimed against the most important—and obvious—figures of authority. A child in a fit might behave very disobediently toward his parents or revile the clergy who came to pray for his recovery. The Reverend Samuel Willard of Groton, who ministered to Elizabeth Knapp during the time of her most severe fits, noted that the Devil "urged upon her constant temptations to murder her p'rents, her neighbors, our children . . . and even to make away with herselfe & once she was going to drowne herself in ye well." The attacking impulses were quite random here, so much so that the girl herself was not safe. Cotton Mather reports a slight variation on this type of behavior in connection with the fits of Martha Goodwin. She would, he writes, "fetch very terrible Blowes with her Fist, and Kicks with her Foot at the man that prayed; but still . . . her Fist and Foot would alwaies recoil, when they came within a few hairs breadths of him just as if Rebounding against a Wall." This little paradigm of aggression attempted and then at the last moment inhibited expresses perfectly the severe inner conflict that many of these people were acting out.

One last, pervasive theme in witchcraft is more difficult to handle than the others without having direct recourse to clinical models; the summary word for it is orality. It is helpful to recall at this point the importance of feats in the standard imaginary picture of witches, but the experience of the accusers speaks even more powerfully to the same point. The evidence is of several kinds. First, the character of the "tortures" inflicted by the witches was most often described in terms of biting, pinching, and pricking; in a psychiatric sense, these modes of attack all have an oral foundation. The pattern showed up with great vividness, for example, in the trial of George Burroughs:

> It was Remarkable that whereas Biting was one of the ways which the Witches used for the vexing of the Sufferers, when they cry'd out of G.B. biting them, the print of the Teeth would be seen on the Flesh of the Complainers, and just such a sett of Teeth at G.B.'s would then appear upon them, which could be distinguished from those of some other mens.

Second, the accusers repeatedly charged that they could see the witches suckling certain animal "familiars." The following testimony by one of the Salem girls, in reference to an unidentified witch, was quite typical: "She had two little things like young cats and she put them to her brest and suckled them they had no hair on them and had ears like a man." It was assumed that witches were specially equipped for these purposes, and their bodies were searched for the evidence. In 1656 the constable of Salisbury, New Hampshire, deposed in the case of Eunice Cole,

> That being about to stripp [her] to bee whipt (by the judgment of the Court att Salisbury) lookeing uppon hir brests under one of hir brests (I thinke hir left brest) I saw a blew thing like unto a teate hanging downeward about three quarters of an inche longe not very thick, and haveing a great suspition in my mind about it (she being suspected for a witche) desired the Court to sende some women to looke of it.

The court accepted this proposal and appointed a committee of three women to administer to Goodwife Cole the standard, very intimate, examination. Their report made no mention of a "teate" under her breast, but noted instead "a place in her leg which was proveable wher she Had bin sucktt by Imps or the like." The women also stated "thatt they Heard the whining of puppies or such like under Her Coats as though they Had a desire to sucke."

Third, many of the accusers underwent serious eating disturbances during and after their fits. "Long fastings" were frequently imposed on them. Cotton Mather writes of one such episode in his account of the bewitching of Margaret Rule: "tho she had a very eager Hunger upon her Stomach, yet if any refreshment were brought unto her, her teeth would be set, and she would be thrown into many Miseries.'' But also she would ''sometimes have her Jaws forcibly pulled open, whereupon something invisible would be poured down her throat. . . . She cried out of it as of Scalding Brimstone poured into her.'' These descriptions and others like them would repay a much more detailed analysis than can be offered here, but the general point should be obvious. Among the zones of the body, the mouth seems to have been charged with special kind of importance for victims of witchcraft.

In closing, it may be appropriate to offer a few suggestions of a more theoretical nature to indicate both the way in which an interpretation of New England witchcraft might be attempted and what it is that one can hope to learn from witchcraft materials about the culture at large. But let it be said with some emphasis that this is meant only as the most tentative beginning of a new approach to such questions.

Consider an interesting set of findings included by two anthropologists in a broad survey of child-rearing in over fifty cultures around the world. They report that belief in witchcraft is powerfully correlated with the training a society imposes on young children in regard to the control of aggressive impulses. That is, wherever this training is severe and restrictive, there is a strong likelihood that the culture will make much of witchcraft. The correlation seems to suggest that suppressed aggression will seek indirect outlets of the kind that belief in witchcraft provides. Unfortunately there is relatively little concrete evidence about child-rearing practices in early New England; but it seems at least consistent with what is known of Puritan culture generally to imagine that quite a harsh attitude would have been taken toward any substantial show of aggression in the young.

Now, some further considerations. There were only a very few cases of witchcraft accusations among members of the same family But, as we have seen, the typical pattern involved accusations by adolescent girls against middle-aged women. It seems plausible, at least from a clinical standpoint, to think that this pattern masked deep problems stemming ultimately from the relationship of mother and daughter. Perhaps, then, the afflicted girls were both projecting their aggression and diverting or ''displacing'' it from its real target. Considered from this perspective, displacement represents another form of avoidance or denial; and so the charges of the accusers may be seen as a kind of double defense against the actual conflicts.

How can we locate the source of these conflicts? This is a more difficult and frankly speculative question. Indeed the question leads farther and farther from the usual canons of historical explanation; such proof as there is must come by way of parallels to findings of recent psychological research and, above all, to a great mass of clinical data. More specifically, it is to psychoanalytic theory that one may turn for insights of an especially helpful sort.

The prominence of oral themes in the historical record suggests that the distubances that culminated in charges of witchcraft must be traced to the earliest phase of personality development. It would be very convenient to have some shred of informaton to insert here about breast-feeding practices among early New Englanders. Possibly their methods of weaning were highly traumatic, but as no hard evidence exists we simply cannot be sure. It seems plausible, however, that many New England children were faced with some unspecified but extremely difficult psychic tasks in the first year or so of life. The outcome was that their aggressive drives were tied especially closely to the oral mode and driven underground. Years later, in accordance with changes normal for adolescence, instinctual energies of all types were greatly augmented; and this tended, as it so often does, to reactivate the earliest conflicts—the process that Freud vividly described as "the return of the repressed." But these conflicts were no easier to deal with in adolescence than they had been earlier; hence the need for the twin defenses of projection and displacement.

One final problem must be recognized. The conflicts on which this discussion has focused were, of course, most vividly expressed in the fits of the accusers. The vast majority of people in early New England—subjected, one assumes, to roughly similar influences as children—managed to reach adulthood without experiencing fits. Does this pose serious difficulties for the above interpretations? The question can be argued to a negative conclusion, in at least two different but complementary ways. First, the materials on witchcraft, and in particular on the fits of the accusers, span a considerable length of time in New England's early history. It seems clear, therefore, that aggression and orality were more or less constant themes in the pathology of the period. Second, even in the far less bizarre testimonies of the witnesses— those who have been taken to represent the community at large—the same sort of focus appears. It is, above all, significant that the specific complaints of the accusers were so completely credible to so many others around them. The accusers, then, can be viewed as those individuals who were somehow especially sensitive to the problems created by their environment; they were the ones who were pushed over the line, so to speak, into serious illness. But their behavior clearly struck an answering chord in a much larger group of people. In this sense, nearly everyone in seventeenth-century New England was at some level an accuser.

KAI T. ERIKSON (b. 1931), a professor of sociology at Yale University, believes that the way in which a society defines and deals with criminality reveals much about the fundamental nature of that society. In his book Wayward Puritans, *Erikson uses the seventeenth century Massachusetts Bay colony as a "laboratory" to test theories about criminal behavior. He notes that episodes of witchcraft were treated relatively lightly in New England prior to the outbreak at Salem. But in 1692 the suggestion that witches were active in Salem triggered a frenzied effort to crush the threat. Why this remarkable change? Erikson argues that by 1692 the faith of the Puritans in their divine mission was eroding. By imagining a conspiracy in their midst, and by moving to punish the conspirators, New Englanders were seeking to restore the sense of common purpose they had lost.*

14. Witchcraft and Social Disruption

Between the end of the Quaker persecutions in 1665 and the beginning of the Salem witchcraft outbreak in 1692, the colony had experienced some very trying days. To begin with, the political outlines of the commonwealth had been subject to sudden, often violent, shifts, and the people of the colony were quite uncertain about their own future. The King's decrees during the Quaker troubles had provoked only minor changes in the actual structure of the Puritan state, but they had introduced a note of apprehension and alarm which did not disappear for thirty years; and no sooner had Charles warned the Massachusetts authorities of his new interest in their affairs then he dispatched four commissioners to the Bay to look after his remote dominions and make sure that his occasional orders were being enforced. From that moment, New England feared the worst. The sermons of the period were full of dreadful prophecies about the future of the Bay, and as New England moved through the 1670's and 1680's, the catalogue of political calamities grew steadily longer and more serious. In 1670, for example, a series of harsh arguments occurred between groups of magistrates and Clergymen, threatening the alliance which had been the very cornerstone of the New England Bay. In 1675 a brutal and costly war broke out with a confederacy of Indian tribes led by a wily chief called King Philip. In 1676 Charles II began to review the claims of other persons to lands within the jurisdiction of Massachusetts, and it became increasingly clear that the old charter might be revoked altogether. In 1679 Charles specifically ordered Massachusetts to permit the establishment of an Anglican church in Boston, and in 1684 the people of the

---

Bay had become so pessimistic about the fate of the colony that several towns simply neglected to send Deputies to the General Court. The sense of impending doom reached its peak in 1686. To begin with, the charter which had given the colony its only legal protection for over half a century was vacated by a stroke of the royal pen, and in addition the King sent a Royal Governor to represent his interests in the Bay who was both an Anglican and a man actively hostile to the larger goals of New England. For the moment, it looked as if the holy experiment was over: not only had the settlers lost title to the very land they were standing on, but they ran the very real risk of witnessing the final collapse of the congregational churches they had built at so great a cost.

The settlers were eventually rescued from the catastrophes of 1686, but their margin of escape had been extremely narrow and highly tentative. In 1689 news began to filter into the Bay that William of Orange had landed in England to challenge the House of Stuart, and hopes ran high throughout the colony; but before the people of the Bay knew the outcome of this contest in England, a Boston mob suddenly rose in protest and placed the Royal Governor in chains. Luckily for Massachusetts, William's forces were successful in England and the Boston insurrection was seen as little more than a premature celebration in honor of the new King. Yet for all the furor, little had changed. At the time of the witchcraft hysteria, agents of Massachusetts were at work in London trying to convince William to restore the old charter, or at least to issue a new one giving Massachusetts all the advantages it had enjoyed in the past, but everyone knew that the colony would never again operate under the same autonomy. As the people of the Bay waited to hear about the future of their settlement, then, their anxiety was understandably high.

Throughout this period of political crisis, an even darker cloud was threatening the colony, and this had to do with the fact that a good deal of angry dissension was spreading among the saints themselves. In a colony that depended on a high degree of harmony and group feeling, the courts were picking their way through a maze of land disputes and personal feuds, a complicated tangle of litigations and suits. Moreover, the earnest attempts at unanimity that had characterized the politics of Winthrop's* era were now replaced by something closely resembling open party bickering. When John Josselyn visited Boston in 1668, for instance, he observed that the people were "savagely factious" in their relations with one another and acted more out of jealousy and greed than any sense of religious purpose. And the

---

Editor's note: John Winthrop (1588–1649) was the first governor of the Massachusetts Bay colony.

sermons of the day chose even stronger language to describe the decline in morality which seemed to darken the prospects of New England. The spirit of brotherhood which the original settlers had counted on so heavily had lately diffused into an atmosphere of commercial competition, political contention, and personal bad feeling.

Thus the political architecture which had been fashioned so carefully by the first generation and the spiritual consensus which had been defended so energetically by the second were both disappearing. At the time of the Salem witchcraft mania, most of the familiar landmarks of the New England Way had become blurred by changes in the historical climate, like signposts obscured in a storm, and the people of the Bay no longer knew how to assess what the past had amounted to or what the future promised. Massachusetts had become, in Alan Heimert's words, "a society no longer able to judge itself with any certainty."

In 1670, the House of Deputies took note of the confusion and fear which was beginning to spread over the country and prepared a brief inventory of the troubles facing the Bay:

> Declension from the primitive foundation work, innovation in doctrine and worship, opinion and practice, an invasion of the rights, liberties and privileges of churches, an usurpation of a lordly and prelatical power over God's heritage, a subversion of the gospel order, and all this with a dangerous tendency to the utter devastation of these churches, turning the pleasant gardens of Christ into a wilderness, and the inevitable and total extirpation of the principles and pillars of the congregational way; these are the leaven, the corrupting gangrene, the infecting spreading plague, the provoking image of jealousy set up before the Lord, the accursed thing which hath provoked divine wrath, and doth further threaten destruction.

The tone of this resolution gives us an excellent index to the mode of the time. For the next twenty years, New England turned more and more to the notion that the settlers must expect God to turn upon them in wrath because the colony had lost its original fervor and sense of mission. The motif introduced in this resolution runs like a recurrent theme through the thinking of the period: the settlers who had carved a commonwealth out of the wilderness and had planted "the pleasant gardens of Christ" in its place were about to return to the wilderness. But there is an important shift of imagery here, for the wilderness they had once mastered was one of thick underbrush and wild animals, dangerous seasons and marauding Indians, while the wilderness which awaited them contained an entirely different sort of peril. "The Wilderness thro' which we are passing to the Promised Land," Cotton Mather wrote in a volume describing the state of New England at the time of the witchcraft difficulties, "is all over fill'd with Fiery flying serpents. . . . All our way to Heaven, lies by the Dens of Lions, and the Mounts of Leopards; there are incredible Droves of Devils in our way." We will return to discussion of this wilderness theme at the conclusion of the chapter, but for the moment it is important to note that Massachusetts had lost much of its concern for institutions and policies and had begun to seek some vision of its future by looking into a ghostly, invisible world.

It was while the people of the colony were preoccupied with these matters that the witches decided to strike.

* * *

Historically, there is nothing unique in the fact that Massachusetts Bay should have put people on trial for witchcraft. As the historian Kittredge has pointed out, the whole story should be seen "not as an abnormal outbreak of fanaticism, not as an isolated tragedy, but as a mere incident, a brief and transitory episode in the biography of a terrible, but perfectly natural, superstition."

The idea of witchcraft, of course, is as old as history; but the concept of a malevolent witch who makes a compact with Satan and rejects God did not appear in Europe until the middle of the fourteenth century and does not seem to have made a serious impression on England until well into the sixteenth. The most comprehensive study of English witchcraft, for example, opens with the year 1558, the first year of Elizabeth's reign, and gives only passing attention to events occurring before that date.

In many ways, witchcraft was brought into England on the same current of change that introduced the Protestant Reformation, and it continued to draw nourishment from the intermittent religious quarrels which broke out during the next century and a half. Perhaps no other form of crime in history has been a better index to social disruption and change, for outbreaks of witchcraft mania have generally taken place in societies which are experiencing a shift of religious focus—societies, we would say, confronting a relocation of boundaries. Throughout the Elizabethan and early Stuart periods, at any rate, while England was trying to establish a national church and to anchor it in the middle of the violent tides which were sweeping over the rest of Europe, increasing attention was devoted to the subject. Elizabeth herself introduced legislation to clarify the laws dealing with witchcraft, and James I, before becoming King of England, wrote a textbook on demonology which became a standard reference for years to come.

But it was during the Civil Wars in England that the witchcraft hysteria struck with full force. Many hundreds, probably thousands of witches were burned or hung between the time the Civil Wars began and Oliver Cromwell emerged as the strong man of the Commonwealth, and no sooner had the mania subsided in England than it broke out all over again in Scotland during the first days of the Restoration. Every important crisis during those years seemed to be punctuated by a rash of witchcraft cases. England did not record its last execution for witchcraft until 1712, but the urgent witch hunts of the Civil War period were never repeated.

With this background in mind, we should not be surprised that New England, too, should experience a moment of panic; but it is rather curious that this moment should have arrived so late in the century.

During the troubled years in England when countless witches were burned at the stake or hung from the gallows, Massachusetts Bay showed but mild concern over the whole matter. In 1647 a witch was executed in Connecticut, and one year later another woman met the same fate in Massachusetts. In 1651 the General Court took note of the witchcraft crisis in England and published an almost laconic order that "a day of humiliation" be observed throughout the Bay, but beyond this, the waves of excitement which were sweeping over the mother country seemed not to reach across the Atlantic at all. There was no shortage of accusations, to be sure, no shortage of the kind of gossip which in other days would send good men and women to their lonely grave, but the magistrates of the colony did not act as if a state of emergency was at hand and thus did not declare a crime wave to be in motion. In 1672, for example, a curious man named John Broadstreet was presented to the Essex County Court for "having familiarity with the devil," yet when he admitted the charge the court was so little impressed that he was fined for telling a lie. And in 1674, when Christopher Brown came before the same court to testify that he had been dealing with Satan, the magistrates flatly dismissed him on the grounds that his confession seemed "inconsistent with truth."

So New England remained relatively calm during the worst of the troubles in England, yet suddenly erupted into a terrible violence long after England lay exhausted from its earlier exertions.

In many important respects, 1692 marked the end of the Puritan experiment in Massachusetts, not only because the original charter had been revoked or because a Royal Governor had been chosen by the King or even because the old political order had collapsed in a tired heap. The Puritan experiment ended in 1692, rather, because the sense of mission which had sustained it from the beginning no longer existed in any recognizable form, and thus the people of the Bay were left with few stable points of reference to help them remember who they were. When they looked back on their own history, the settlers had to conclude that the trajectory of the past pointed in quite a different direction than the one they now found themselves taking: they were no longer participants in a great adventure, no longer residents of a "city upon a hill," no longer members of that special revolutionary elite who were destined to bend the course of history according to God's own word. They were only themselves, living alone in a remote corner of the world, and this seemed a modest end for a crusade which had begun with such high expectations.

In the first place, as we have seen, the people of the colony had always pictured themselves as actors in an international movement, yet by the end of the century they had lost many of their most meaningful contacts with the rest of the world. The Puritan movement in England had scattered into a number of separate sects, each of which had been gradually absorbed into the freer climate of a new regime, and elsewhere in Europe the Protestant Reformation had lost much of its momentum without achieving half the goals set for it. And as a result, the colonists had lost touch with the background against which they had learned to assess their own stature and to survey their own place in the world.

In the second place, the original settlers had measured their achievements on a yardstick which no longer seemed to have the same sharp relevance. New England had been built by people who believed that God personally supervised every flicker of life on earth according to a plan beyond human comprehension, and in undertaking the expedition to America they were placing themselves entirely in God's hands. These were men whose doctrine prepared them to accept defeat gracefully, whose sense of piety depended upon an occasional moment of failure, hardship, even tragedy. Yet by the end of the century, the Puritan planters could look around them and count an impressive number of accomplishments. Here was no record of erratic providence; here was a record of solid human enterprise, and with this realization, as Daniel Boorstin suggests, the settlers moved from a "sense of mystery" to a "consciousness of mastery," from a helpless reliance on fate to a firm confidence in their own abilities. This shift helped clear the way for the appearance of the shrewd, practical, self-reliant Yankee as a figure in American history, but in the meantaime it left the third generation of settlers with no clear definition of the status they held as the chosen children of God.

In the third place, Massachusetts had been founded as a lonely pocket of civilization in the midst of a howling wilderness, and as we have seen, this idea remained one of the most important themes of Puritan imagery long after the underbrush had been cut away and the wild animals killed. The settlers had lost sight of their local frontiers, not only in the sense that colonization had spread beyond the Berkshires into what is now upper state New York, but also in the sense that the wilderness which had held the community together by pressing in on it from all sides was disappearing. The original settlers had landed in a wilderness full of "wild beasts and wilder men"; yet sixty years later, sitting many miles from the nearest frontier in the prosperous seaboard town of Boston, Cotton Mather and other survivors of the old order still imagined that they were living in a wilderness—a territory they had explored as thoroughly as any frontiersmen. But the character of this wilderness was unlike anything the first settlers had ever seen, for its dense forests had become a jungle of mythical beasts and its skies were thick with flying spirits. In a sense, the Puritan community had helped mark its location in space by keeping close watch on the wilderness surrounding it on all sides; and now that the visible traces of that wilderness had receded out of sight, the settlers invented a new one by finding the shapes of the forest in the middle of the community itself.

And as the wilderness took on this new character, it seemed that the Devil had given up his more familiar disguises. He no longer lurked in the underbrush, for most of it had been cut away; he no longer assumed the shape of hostile Indians, for most of them had retreated inland for the moment; he no longer sent waves of heretics to trouble the Bay, for most of them lived quietly under the protection of toleration; he no longer appeared in the armies of the Counter-Reformation, for the old battlefields were still and too far away to excite the imagination. But his presence was felt everywhere, and when the colonists began to look for his new hiding places they found him crouched in the very heart of the Puritan colony. Quite literally, the people of the Bay began to see ghosts, and soon the boundaries of the New England Way closed in on a space full of demons and incubi, spectres and evil spirits, as the settlers tried to find a new sense of their own identity among the landmarks of a strange, invisible world. Cotton Mather, who knew every disguise in the Devil's wardrobe, offered a frightening catalogue of the Devil's attempts to destroy New England.

> I believe, there never was a poor Plantation, more pursued by the wrath of the Devil, than our poor New-England. . . . It was a rousing alarm to the Devil, when a great Company of English Protestants and Puritans, came to erect Evangelical Churches, in a corner of the world, where he had reign'd without control for many ages; and it is a vexing Eye-sore to the Devil, that our Lord Christ should be known, and own'd and preached in this howling wilderness. Wherefore he has left no Stone unturned, that so he might undermine his Plantation, and force us out of our Country.

First, the Indian Powawes, used all their Sorceries to molest the first Planters here; but God said unto them, Touch them not! Then Seducing spirits came to root in this Vineyard, but God so rated them off, that they have not prevail'd much farther than the edges of our Land. After this, we have had a continual blast upon some of our principal Grain, annually diminishing a vast part of our ordinary Food. Herewithal, wasting Sicknesses, especially Burning and Mortal Agues, have Shot the Arrows of Death in at our Windows. Next, we have had many Adversaries of our own Language, who have been perpetually assaying to deprive us of those English Liberties, in the encouragement whereof these Territories have been settled. As if this had not been enough; the Tawnies among whom we came have watered our Soil with the Blood of many Hundreds of Inhabitants. . . . Besides all which, now at last the Devils are (if I may so speak) in Person come down upon us with such a Wrath, as is justly much, and will quickly be more, the Astonishment of the World.

And this last adventure of the Devil has a quality all its own.

Wherefore the Devil is now making one Attempt more upon us; an Attempt more Difficult, more Surprising, more snarl'd with unintelligible Circumstances than any that we have hitherto Encountered. . . . An Army of Devils is horribly broke in upon the place which is the center, and after a sort, the First-born of our English Settlements: and the Houses of the Good People there are fill'd with the doleful shrieks of their Children and Servants, Tormented by Invisible Hands, with Tortures altogether preternatural.

The witchcraft hysteria occupied but a brief moment in the history of the Bay. The first actors to take part in it were a group of excited girls and a few of the less savory figures who drifted around the edges of the community, but the speed with which the other people of the Bay gathered to witness the encounter and accept an active role in it, not to mention the quality of the other persons who were eventually drawn into this vortex of activity, serves as an index to the gravity of the issues involved. For a few years, at least, the settlers of Massachusetts were alone in the world, bewildered by the loss of their old destiny but not yet aware of their new one, and during this fateful interval they tried to discover some image of themselves by listening to a chorus of voices which whispered to them from the depths of an invisible wilderness.

Two historians at the University of Massachusetts, PAUL BOYER (b.1935) and STEPHEN NISSENBAUM (b. 1941), have also brought a new perspective to the study of witchcraft at Salem. Unlike most earlier historians, they are more concerned with the history of the community in the decades that preceded 1692 than with the events of that year.

According to Boyer and Nissenbaum, Salem Village by 1692 was primed for an explosion between two bitterly opposed groups: the supporters and the opponents of the controversial minister, Samuel Parris. These groups formed around two prominent Village families. The Putnams led the pro-Parris faction while the Porters led the dissenters. And behind this hostility between two families was a more fundamental division between two opposing ways of life. The social order of Salem Village, traditionally agrarian and devout, was being threatened by the commercial and secular infuences of the neighboring seaport, Salem Town. When the crisis over witchcraft occurred it followed these same fault lines. The accusers, who came from the pro-Parris faction, translated their resentment against their cosmopolitan enemies into accusations of witchcraft. Boyer and Nissenbaum have written that this conflict affected the lives of individuals on both sides of the Ipswich Road, the thoroughfare that separated Salem Village from Salem Town. Taken from their book Salem Possessed, *the brief excerpt that follows sums up the authors' conclusions.*

15. A Clash of Two Worlds

What we have been attempting through all the preceding chapters is to convey something of the deeper historical resonances of our story while still respecting its uniqueness. We see no real conflict between these two purposes. To be sure, no other community was precisely like Salem Village, and no other men were exactly like embittered Samuel Parris, cool and ambitious Israel Porter, or Thomas Putnam, Jr., grimly watching the steady diminution of his worldly estate.*

This irreducible particularity, these intensely personal aspirations and private fears, fairly leap from the documents these Salem Villagers, and others, left behind them. And had we been able to learn to know them better—heard the timbre of their voices, watched the play of emotion across their faces, observed even a few of those countless moments in their lives which went unrecorded—we might have been able to apprehend with even greater force the pungent flavor of their individuality.

From Paul Boyer and Stephen Nissenbaum, *Salem Possessed: the Social Origins of Witchcraft* (Cambridge, Mass.: Harvard University Press, 1974). Reprinted by permission of the Harvard University Press. Copyright © 1974 by the President and Fellows of Harvard College.

Editor's note: Israel Porter was a well-to-do leader of the faction that opposed Rev. Samuel Parris. Thomas Putnam, Jr., was a leader of the faction supporting the minister.

But the more we have come to know these men for something like what they really were, the more we have also come to realize how profoundly they were shaped by the times in which they lived. For if they were unlike any other men, so was their world unlike any other world before or since; and they shared that world with other people living in other places. Parris and Putnam and the rest were, after all, not only Salem Villagers: they were also men of the seventeenth century; they were New Englanders; and, finally, they were Puritans.

If the large concepts with which historians conventionally deal are to have any meaning, it is only as they can be made manifest in individual cases like these. The problems which confronted Salem Village in fact encompassed some of the central issues of New England society in the late seventeenth century: the resistance of back-country farmers to the pressures of commercial capitalism and the social style that accompanied it; the breaking away of outlying areas from parent towns; difficulties between ministers and their congregations; the crowding of third-generation sons from family lands; the shifting locus of authority within individual communities and society as a whole; the very quality of life in an unsettled age. But for men like Samuel Parris and Thomas Putnam, Jr., these issues were not abstractions. They emerged as upsetting personal encounters with people like Israel Porter and Daniel Andrew, and as unfavorable decisions handed down in places like Boston and Salem Town.*

It was in 1692 that these men for the first time attempted (just as we are attempting in this book) to piece together the shards of their experience, to shape their malaise into some broader theoretical pattern, and to comprehend the full dimensions of those forces which they vaguely sensed were shaping their private destinies. Oddly enough, it has been through our sense of "collaborating" with Parris and the Putnams in their effort to delineate the larger contours of their world, and our sympathy, at least on the level of metaphor, with certain of their perceptions, that we have come to feel a curious bond with the "witch hunters" of 1692.

But one advantage we as outsiders have had over the people of Salem Village is that we can afford to recognize the degree to which the menace they were fighting off had taken root within each of them almost as deeply as it had in Salem Town or along the Ispwich Road. It is at this level, indeed, that we have most clearly come to recognize the implications of their travail for our understanding of what might be called the Puritan temper during that final,

---

Editor's note: Daniel Andrew, who was associated with the anti-Parris faction, was accused of witchcraft in 1692.

often intense, and occasionally lurid efflorescence which signaled the end of its century-long history. For Samuel Parris and Thomas Putnam, Jr., were part of a vast company, on both sides of the Atlantic, who were trying to expunge the lure of a new order from their own souls by doing battle with it in the real world. While this company of Puritans were not the purveyors of the spirit of capitalism that historians once made them out to be, neither were they simple peasants clinging blindly to the imagined security of a receding medieval culture. What seems above all to characterize them, and even to help define their identity as "Puritans," is the precarious way in which they managed to inhabit both these worlds at once.

The inner tensions that shaped the Puritan temper were inherent in it from the very start, but rarely did they emerge with such raw force as in 1692, in little Salem Village. For here was a community in which these tensions were exacerbated by a tangle of external circumstances: a community so situated geographically that its inhabitants experienced two different economic systems, two different ways of life, at unavoidably close range; and so structured politically that it was next to impossible to locate, either within the Village or outside it, a dependable and unambiguous center of authority which might hold in check the effects of these accidents of geography.

The spark which finally set off this volatile mix came with the unlikely convergence of a set of chance factors in the early 1690's: the arrival of a new minister who brought with him a slave acquainted with West Indian voodoo lore; the heightened interest throughout New England in fortune telling and the occult, taken up in Salem Village by an intense group of adolescent girls related by blood and faction to the master of that slave; the coming-of-age of Joseph Putnam, who bore the name of one of Salem Village's two controlling families while owing his allegiance to the other; the political and legal developmments in Boston and London which hamstrung provincial authorities for several crucial months early in 1692.

But beyond these proximate causes lie the deeper and more inexorable ones we have already discussed. For in the witchcraft outburst of Salem Village, perhaps the most exceptional event in American colonial history, certainly the most bizarre, one finds laid bare the central concerns of the era.

Suggestions for Further Reading

(Books available in paperback editions are marked with an asterisk)

The literature on the outbreak of witchcraft at Salem is vast, but the literature on witchcraft in general is vaster still. A good introduction to the entire field from an anthropological perspective is *Witchcraft*★ by Lucy Mair (New York, 1969). *Witchcraft and Sorcery*★ edited by Max Marwick (Baltimore, 1970) is a collection of essays by historians, anthropologists, and sociologists. A classic study of witchcraft in a non-Western society is *Witchcraft, Oracles, and Magic Among the Azande*★ by E. E. Evans-Pritchard (Oxford, 1937).

For the historical study of witchcraft, which primarily means Europe between 1500 and 1700, two recent books on England are outstanding: *Witchcraft in Tudor and Stuart England*★ by A. D. J. MacFarlane (London, 1970) and *Religion and the Decline of Magic*★ by Keith Thomas (New York, 1971). Two studies broader in scope, but somewhat idiosyncratic, are *The World of the Witches*★ by Julio Caro Baroja (Chicago, 1975) and *The European Witch-Craze of the Sixteenth and Seventeenth Century*★ by H. R. Trevor-Roper (New York, 1968). For a detailed bibliography of historical studies, see H. C. Erik Midelfort, "Recent Witchhunting Research," *Papers of the American Bibliographic Society,* vol. 62 (1968), pp. 373–418.

Several collections exist of original sources on Salem witchcraft. The most readily available are two anthologies which mix legal records with literary sources: *What Happened in Salem*★ edited by David Levin (New York, 1960) and *Salem Village Witchcraft*★ edited by Paul Boyer and Stephen Nissenbaum (Belmont, Calif., 1972). An earlier collection of literary sources, including works by Cotton Mather and Robert Calef, is *Narratives of the Witchcraft Cases* edited by George L. Burr (New York, 1914). For the trial records, see *Records of Salem Witchcraft* (2 vols., Roxbury, Mass., 1864). A typescript of the trial records was also made by the Works Progress Administration in 1938. A new collection of the trial records which is more accurate than the 1864 edition and more readily available than the WPA typescript is Paul Boyer and Stephen Nissenbaum (editors) *The Salem Witchcraft Papers* (3 vols., New York, 1977).

In regard to the writings of historians on Salem, perhaps the first genuine attempt to arrive at an objective view was *The History of the Colony and Province of Massachusetts-Bay* (Cambridge, Mass., 1936), written in 1750 by Thomas Hutchinson, who had known some of the principal actors in the outbreak. The classic historical account was *Salem Witchcraft* by Charles W. Upham (2 vols., Boston, 1867). An early critic of Upham, William Frederick Poole, published his counterattack "Cotton Mather and Salem Witchcraft," in *North American Review,* CVIII (1869), pp. 337–397. Another nineteenth century writer who differed with Upham was Barrett Wendell. His experience with spiritualists prompted him to write "Were the Salem Witches Guiltless?" *Historical Collections of the Essex Institute,* XXIX (1892), pp. 129–147. In the twentieth century, the argument that some of the witches were guilty has been advanced with greater persuasiveness in *Witchcraft at Salem** by Chadwick Hansen (New York, 1969).

Several writers have explored the psychological aspects of Salem. The pioneering American psychologist George M. Beard speculated on this subject in *Psychology of the Salem Witchcraft Excitement* (New York, 1882). Although it is interesting reading, this book is of little use to the modern student of witchcraft. Similarly, the opinion of John Fiske in his *New France and New England* (New York, 1902) that the girls suffered a "contagion of hysterical emotion" is unsophisticated by today's standards. A more recent view is Marion L. Starkey, *The Devil in Massachusetts** (New York, 1949). This popular, well-written account draws on psychological literature. Perhaps the most convincing psychological interpretation comes in Chadwick Hansen, *Witchcraft at Salem.**

A good deal of ink has been used attacking and defending the Puritan role in Salem. In the seventeenth century, Cotton Mather traded charges with Robert Calef. In the eighteenth century, W. F. Poole attacked Charles W. Upham over the same issue. This debate continued in the twentieth century. On one side were those who scoffed at the Puritan tradition as anti-democratic and anti-rationalist. In *The Founding of New England* by James Truslow Adams (Boston, 1921), Salem was used as an example of Puritan intolerance. The counterattack, when it came, was lead by historians from Harvard. Samuel Eliot Morison, in *The Intellectual Life of Puritan New England** (New York, 1936), tried to achieve a more sympathetic view of the Puritan attitude toward witchcraft. Perry Miller, also of Harvard, treated the witchcraft episode with understanding in *The New England Mind: From Colony to Province** (Cambridge, Mass., 1953). Miller also discussed this issue in an anthology co-edited with Thomas H. Johnson, *The Puritans** (2 vols., New York, 1938). For a recent study of the arch-Puritan Cotton Mather and his family see Robert Middlekauf, *The Mathers: Three Generations of Puritan Intellectuals*★ (New York, 1971).

The criminological aspects of Salem are discussed in two books, one by a sociologist and the other by a professor of law. Kai T. Erikson's *Wayward Puritans*★ (New York, 1966), concerns the "sociology of deviance" in seventeenth century Massachusetts, and includes a discussion of witchcraft. *Science and Justice* by Sanford J. Fox (Baltimore, 1968) examines the use of science in the legal proceedings against the witches.

Two recent works examine the spread of occult lore in the American colonies: Herbert Leventhal, *In the Shadow of the Enlightenment* (New York, 1976) and Jon Butler, "Magic, Astrology, and the Early American Religious Heritage," *American Historical Review,* 84 (April, 1979, pp. 317–346.